www.ingramcontent.com/pod-product-compliance
Lightning Source LLC
Chambersburg PA
CBHW081439090426
42740CB00017B/3362

Contents

Chapter One: Introduction

Welcome to *The Legends of Acoustic Guitar*.

In my previous two books, *The Tradition* and *The Heritage*, I created solo fingerstyle guitar arrangements that were designed to stand alone. For this book, I decided to travel a different route and look at the acoustic guitar styles and techniques of the great singer-songwriters.

It struck me that, as acoustic and fingerstyle guitarists, we spend a lot of our time playing unaccompanied. This is a great skill to develop but can lead to problems along the way. Often, we will develop our own sense of "internal time" that strays far more than we realise. While researching the artists for this book, I was repeatedly struck by how great they were at keeping time with other musicians. Some (like Paul Simon) are adept at keeping the timing rock solid while accompanying just one other musician. Indeed, when it came to recording these pieces, I was reminded how much I need to work on strengthening my own timing when playing to a fixed rhythm!

There is a huge amount we can learn from great singer-songwriters: their parts are frequently creative and designed to complement their vocal part/melody lines, sitting perfectly within a band context. As acoustic guitarists we often find ourselves leaving the realm of solo performance and playing with other musicians, so knowing *what to play* and *when to play it* are crucial skills to develop.

While the pieces in this book are not as complex as those found in my earlier books, there are still inherent challenges – not least, to capture the personality and (in some instances) idiosyncrasies of the players. Delving into the styles of these players will pay dividends for your playing technique and accompaniment/arrangement skills. From the flowing intros of James Taylor to the percussive, driving style of Mark Knopfler, you are certain to find new ideas that will filter into your guitar style – I certainly did!

I hope you enjoy learning and playing these pieces and if you have any questions, please don't hesitate to contact me at **stuart@stuartryanmusic.com**

Stuart Ryan

Bath, UK, February 2020

Dedications

To my beautiful wife, Cori, for always encouraging me and supporting me in these projects. Teddy the Labrador, for not knocking over any microphones on the few occasions I allowed him in to be "Studio dog" and for keeping the barking to a minimum during critical recording sessions. Mum and Dad for starting the guitar journey almost thirty years ago. Neville Marten and Jason Sidwell and *Guitar Techniques* magazine, David Mead and Jamie Dickson at *Guitarist* magazine. Stuart Clayton for design and layout, James Uings for all the audio advice, Noel Sheehan and Nick Campling at G7th capos. To my guitar friends Jon Gomm, Thomas Leeb, Declan Zapala and John Wheatcroft.

Get the Audio

The audio files for this book are available to download for free from **www.fundamental-changes.com.** The link is in the top right-hand corner. Simply select this book title from the drop-down menu and follow the instructions to get the audio.

We recommend that you download the files directly to your computer, not to your tablet, and extract them there before adding them to your media library. You can then put them on your tablet, iPod or burn them to CD. On the download page there is a help PDF and we also provide technical support via the contact form.

For over 350 Free Guitar Lessons with Videos Check out:

www.fundamental-changes.com

Over 11,000 fans on Facebook: **FundamentalChangesInGuitar**

Instagram: **FundamentalChanges**

Chapter Two: Overview

I chose to study a diverse range of players for this book. They are all drawn from the world of Pop/Rock but have something different to offer. We will examine the style of each artist in detail in the chapters that follow, and I have suggested essential pieces to learn alongside the example track, but first here is an overview of what to expect from each artist and how to approach their style.

How to use this book

I've designed these pieces to be approached in a number of different ways:

• You can learn and re-create the parts as a way of working on your timing, clarity and accuracy

• You can adapt the written parts to introduce some of your own style alongside that of the original artist

• Use the backing tracks to invent your own unique parts – either in the style of the original artist or using your own approach

What we can learn from the players

Mark Knopfler – While he came to prominence as the Strat/Les Paul-wielding front man of Dire Straits, the acoustic guitar and fingerstyle technique have always been prominent in Knopfler's playing and writing. Even when playing electric, he eschews the pick in favour of his fingers, which is one of the elements that yields his incredible electric guitar sound. Over the course of his solo career the acoustic guitar seems to have taken over as the main instrument in his playing and writing. His distinctive style features a powerful attack and, on some pieces, a combined "pick and flick" approach that gives his playing a driving, percussive quality.

Bruce Springsteen – Like Knopfler, "The Boss" is another artist who conjures up the image of an electric guitar toting troubadour for most people. But while his famous butterscotch Fender Telecaster drove many of his biggest hits, the acoustic guitar has been at the heart of his style from day one. Early albums like *Nebraska* reveal an artist who uses the acoustic guitar as the tool of choice when it comes to song writing. Over the years the steel string has really come to prominence in his writing and performing and some albums contain far more acoustic than electric. Springsteen is a fan of alternate tunings and crafts his distinctively Americana-inspired parts using a variety of dropped tunings. For this study we will be in "double dropped D" which gives the guitar a big, meaty sound, perfectly suited to Springsteen's percussive strumming style.

James Taylor – Taylor famously uses some unorthodox fingerings for his guitar parts that can make them notoriously difficult to learn, especially if you are aiming to exactly replicate what he does! Luckily, you don't need to take that approach for this study (although you are of course welcome to). His flowing, arpeggiated parts are so perfectly woven into everything he does that they can occupy centre stage while still providing the perfect backdrop for his wonderful voice. Taylor is also the master of the melodic intro – a short, unaccompanied figure that serves to open the piece before the band enters. It's worth learning all of these parts on their own to get a sense of just how melodic he is.

George Harrison – Often regarded as the "Quiet Beatle", for me Harrison was the most creative guitarist in the group. His writing was always super-melodic and the guitar drove his pieces with remarkable fluidity. The study in this book shows how the use of a capo can be so important in making a guitar part really stand out.

You can approach this piece either with a pick or fingerstyle. It's worth practising both to see the benefits/ drawbacks of each method. Aim for clean, rhythmic playing on this one but don't worry too much if you find yourself straying a little from the written parts!

Neil Young – Over the course of a long and varied career, Young has veered from pastoral Americana to face melting, feedback driven electric guitar. For the study in this book I've focused on the gentle, melodic strumming style he used during the *Harvest Moon* period. Young is a fan of alternate tunings and for this piece I opted for drop D. This is of particular benefit when working in the key of D as the lower pitch on string 6 tends to give the guitar a "bigger" sound overall and strummed parts can really create a lot of space and depth within a track. At other times Young uses a heavily percussive strummed style, but here it is all about a gentle, even approach to keep the chords consistent and allow everything to ring out as much as possible so that the guitar fills out the track.

Tracy Chapman – While her guitar parts are not complex, Chapman is a great example of how the acoustic guitar can fit into a Pop/Rock context as both the driving force of the track and also a rhythmic tool. There are some great contrasts within her playing: she will move from open position fingerpicked chords using some embellishments for added colour, to "thinner" melodic parts higher up the fretboard that bring to mind Paul McCartney's ideas in *Blackbird*. Moving from delicate fingerpicking to driving strumming is an essential skill for any acoustic player. In the recording studio you would most likely record fingerpicked parts separately to strumming, but a useful skill to learn is to keep the pick tucked in the fingers while fingerpicking, then quickly release it to be available for strummed sections. Of course, you can strum with the picking hand fingers, but the pick hold/release technique is great as it will usually give you a more consistent strummed part.

John Mayer – Another huge star commonly seen with an electric guitar (usually a Strat, though increasingly anything else he can get his hands on), Mayer has been crafting his art with the acoustic guitar from day one. His first EP, *Inside Wants Out*, was dominated by acoustic guitar and early tracks like *Neon* feature his virtuoso fingerstyle playing, which would stand on its own even without his vocal lines. In recent years the acoustic has returned to the fore on his album releases and the last few have seen him tipping his hat to the classic Country/ Americana sounds of Crosby, Stills and Nash, Bob Dylan and Neil Young. For this study we see how he takes these influences and stamps his own distinctive approach on them.

Noel Gallagher – Although not generally revered as a guitarist, Gallagher is a great example of how the acoustic guitar can underpin a track allowing the melody and vocals to take centre stage. However, while Gallagher writes within conventional song-form structures, it's the colour he adds to standard progressions that make his parts of interest. His use of minor 7 and add 9 chords make his strumming parts instantly memorable, and that bit more sophisticated compared to many of his peers. This study is not challenging but provides a great opportunity to work on dynamic, rhythmic playing within a Rock context.

Paul Simon – A master accompanist, Simon has in effect had two careers, starting in the duo format with Art Garfunkel, then continuing with a long solo career which has taken in everything from American traditional Folk to the sounds of Africa and Brazil. Simon's style is derived from the 1960's Greenwich Village approach (via the London Soho café scene of the same era). For this study I wanted to take a look at his more sophisticated approach to harmony, so this piece contains some interesting Jazz/Gospel chord work. There is some great footage of him performing *Still Crazy After All These Years* whilst still in the writing stage; a quick search on YouTube will yield the relevant result.

Joni Mitchell – Mitchell has a unique approach to the guitar which she herself has described as, "me not being able to play like Elizabeth Cotton" – one of her earliest influences. As a result, she developed a highly

individualistic style and the vast majority of her compositions feature alternate tunings, sometimes lush Jazz-influenced chords, and a harp-like picking style. Our study will feature one of her favourite tunings of CGDFCE and highlight her controlled use of dissonance in her song writing.

Audio Production Notes

All audio for this book is produced, engineered and mastered by Stuart Ryan. I used a Gibson J35 Collector's edition for all tracks except the John Mayer-style track, which is played on my wonderful Circa 000, built by gifted luthier John Slobod. The microphones used were a Brauner Phanthera and Telefunken M260; mic preamps were a Chandler TG500, Heritage Audio 73 'Jr and Buzz Audio Elixir. Most tracks featured guitars recorded in stereo with a combination of mic placements – normally the Brauner at the 12th fret and the Telefunken in the "over the shoulder" position or the Telefunken pointing at the 12th fret and the Brauner pointing towards the bridge, positioned above the upper bout and pointing downwards.

Audio was recorded into Logic X using Apogee converters. I used a number of plug-ins, but some standouts are the Maag EQ4, Fab Filter Eq and Kush Audio Clariphonic.

Chapter Three: Mark Knopfler

Artist Overview

Born in Glasgow, Scotland, in 1949, Mark Knopfler's early influences were actually boogie woogie piano players. However, as a child, seeing Hank Marvin and that famous red Fender Stratocaster strengthened his burgeoning interest in guitar. His early guitar influences came from several musical backgrounds: the country style of Chet Atkins and Scotty Moore, the blues of BB King and the Gypsy Jazz of Django Reinhardt. You can hear elements of these disparate influences in much of his playing with a particularly strong pull to the country side of things (remember those famous *Sultans of Swing* solos).

Although he is synonymous with iconic electric guitar riffs such as *Money for Nothing* and the blistering solos on *Sultans of Swing*, the acoustic guitar and fingerpicking have always been a huge part of Mark Knopfler's guitar style – so much so, that his electric guitar playing is actually driven by his fingerstyle technique. A masterful fingerpicker, Knopfler's unique style is partly characterized by the interplay between picking hand thumb and index finger. His picking hand *groove* will form the subject of this lesson. What's more, you don't get to record an album with Chet Atkins (check out *Neck and Neck*) unless your fingerstyle chops are up to par!

The acoustic was always a feature of Dire Straits' music (remember the famous fingerpicked Dobro lines in *Romeo and Juliet,* for example), but it is in Knopfler's solo career that the acoustic has really come to the fore. Although you will often see him using a standard fingerpicking approach for arpeggiating chords, he also frequently utilizes an altogether different technique for building pulsing, percussive acoustic guitar parts. His approach in this scenario involves a technique that is closer to banjo "frailing". In essence, this involves picking a note with the thumb and following this with a note that is "flicked" with the nail of the index or middle finger. In order to make sufficient impact on the string, you need to curl the finger into the palm of the hand (I favour the picking hand middle finger), then flick it onto the string with one fast, fluid movement. If you achieve enough impact, you'll get the required percussive sound on the string and the finger will bounce back off the string. Sometimes the flicked note is then rapidly followed by another note, which is sounded by an upstroke with the index finger.

Listen and Learn: *The Man's Too Strong, Redbud Tree, Sailing to Philadelphia.*

Performance Notes

General Overview

At first glance it may appear that you should approach this piece with a plectrum, but there are two reasons for not doing so. Firstly, it is necessary to incorporate some of Knopfler's technique into your playing in order to give this part its percussive, driving sound. Secondly, you will need to use your picking hand fingers for the arpeggiated parts which appear later on in the piece.

Bar 1 – This simple E minor chord won't pose any challenges for the fretting hand, leaving you to work on the necessary picking hand technique. In order to achieve the powerful "thwack" first pick the bass note on the open E with the picking hand thumb, then flick the nail of the middle finger down onto strings 4, 3 and 2. This should be done with a rapid motion resulting in the nail of this finger bouncing off strings 4, 3 and 2. You can also flick downwards with the nail side of the index, middle and ring fingers, which will give a percussive sound if you flick hard and fast enough. Resist the temptation to pluck these three strings with those fingers, however, as the will soften the sound dramatically.

Bar 2 – The picking hand pattern becomes a bit more complex here. Start with the picking hand thumb followed by the middle finger as covered in Bar 1. On beat three, use a downstroke with the thumb followed by the hammer-on. The challenges come on beat four, where you flick the chord using the back of the middle finger nail as discussed; then, to play the last chord in this bar, quickly flick the index finger upwards over the strings. Getting the balance of timing and volume right is a challenge, so to begin with I would loop this two-bar sequence very slowly until it sounds smooth and even. The down and upstrokes are indicated beneath the picking hand fingering.

Bar 15 – This sequence is effectively a fill that takes us back to the start of the piece. Getting it right depends on using the correct sequence of picking hand fingers as outlined. We are still using downstrokes on the thumb, the nail flick on the middle finger, and the upstroke on the index finger, but there is more going on now. Build this sequence very slowly using the fingerings indicated and remember to keep the middle finger and index finger flick rapid and strong.

Bar 18 – These picking hand techniques work all over the neck. We are now using the same ideas, but on the A Major chord and all that follows.

Bar 34 – Here the part changes to a more traditional fingerpicked approach. You can approach this using the standard *pima* picking hand patterns, where the thumb (*p*) takes care of strings 6, 5 and 4 and the index (*i*), middle (*m*) and ring (*a*) fingers take care of strings 3, 2 and 1 respectively. However, if you want to practise the "thumb and flick" approach, then keep it going here. Use the thumb to pluck the note on beat one, then sound the chord on beat two, either with a downward flick from the middle finger or a downward flick using the index, middle and ring fingers together.

Bar 36 – The easiest way to sound this sequence is to use the thumb to pluck the bass notes on beats one and three and a downward flick on the chords using relaxed index, middle and ring fingers together.

Bar 58 – This bluesy outro lick is a great opportunity to practise picking lead lines with the fingers. Try using my suggested picking hand fingering and remember to make the legato (hammer-ons and pull-offs) strong and smooth, so all the notes sound evenly and in time.

Shopping List

Knopfler has a guitar collection to turn any gear nut weak at the knees, with many priceless, vintage pieces to drool over. There have been several Martin Mark Knopfler signature models over the years from the OOO (smaller body) to an HD40 (dreadnought). He has also been seen with old Gibsons amongst others. Anything goes for this style, but something with a lively response will help bring out the percussive elements more.

♩ = 202
Tuning = EADGBE

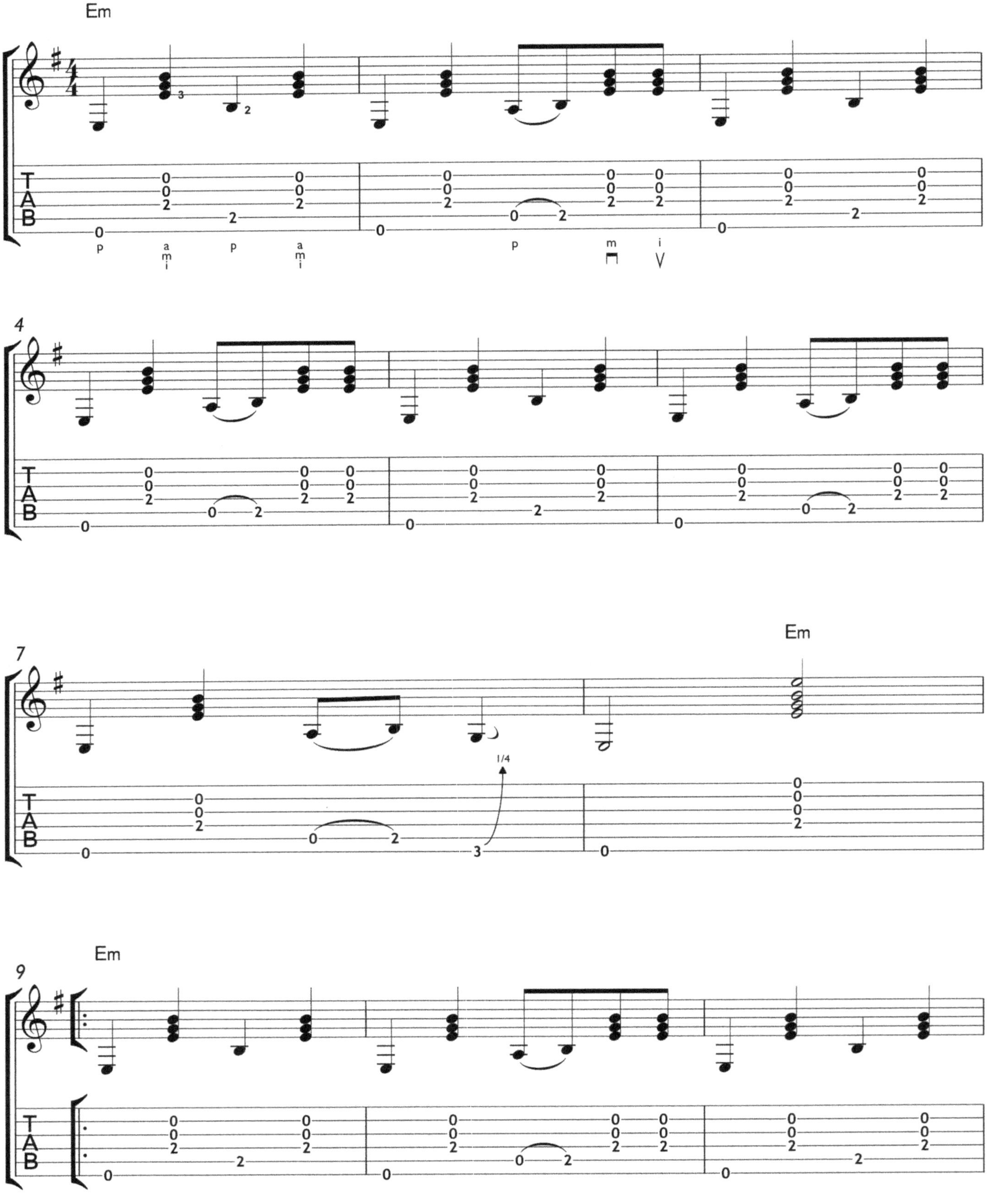

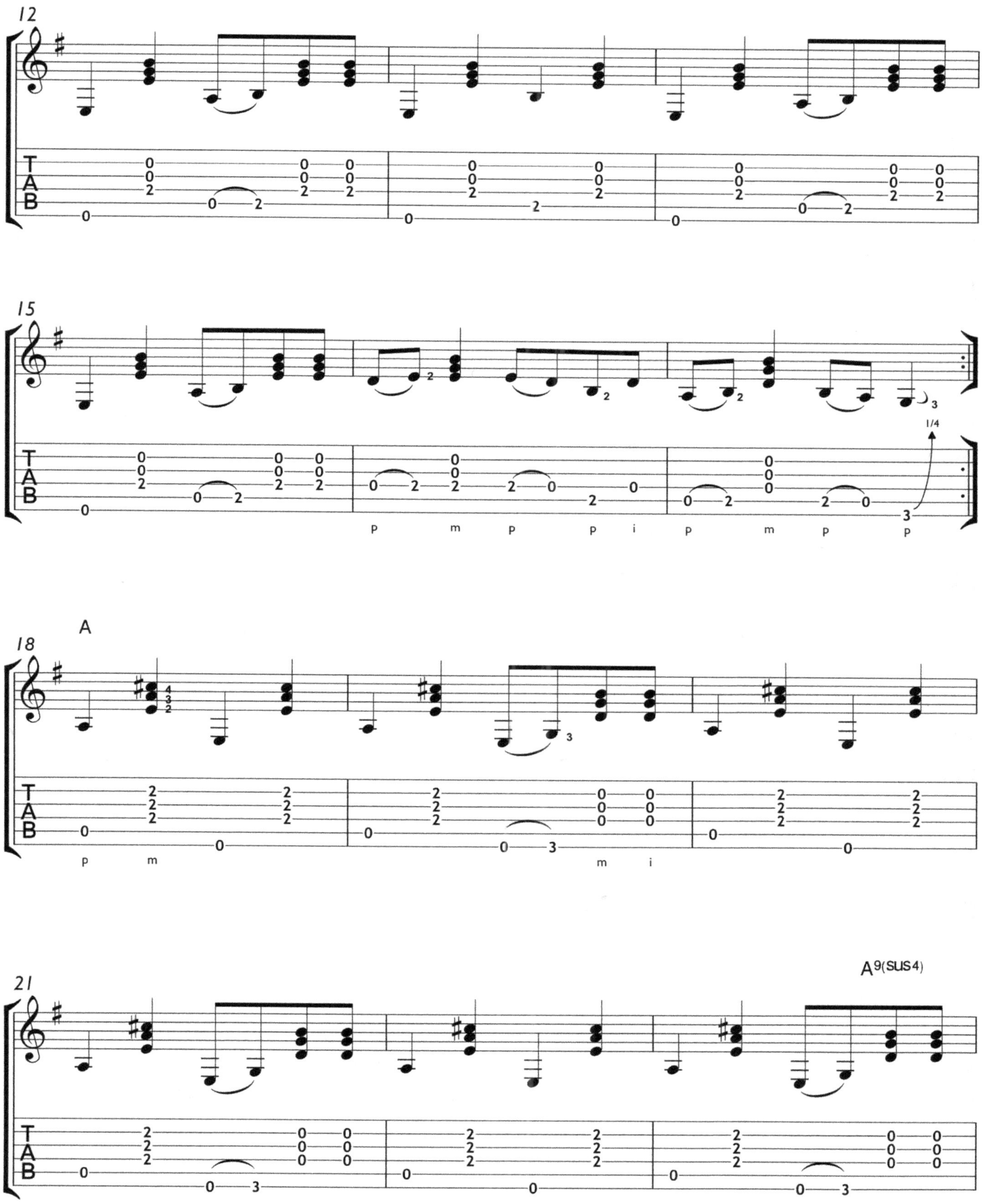
12
15
1/4
p m p p i p m p p
A
18
p m
m i
21
A9(SUS4)

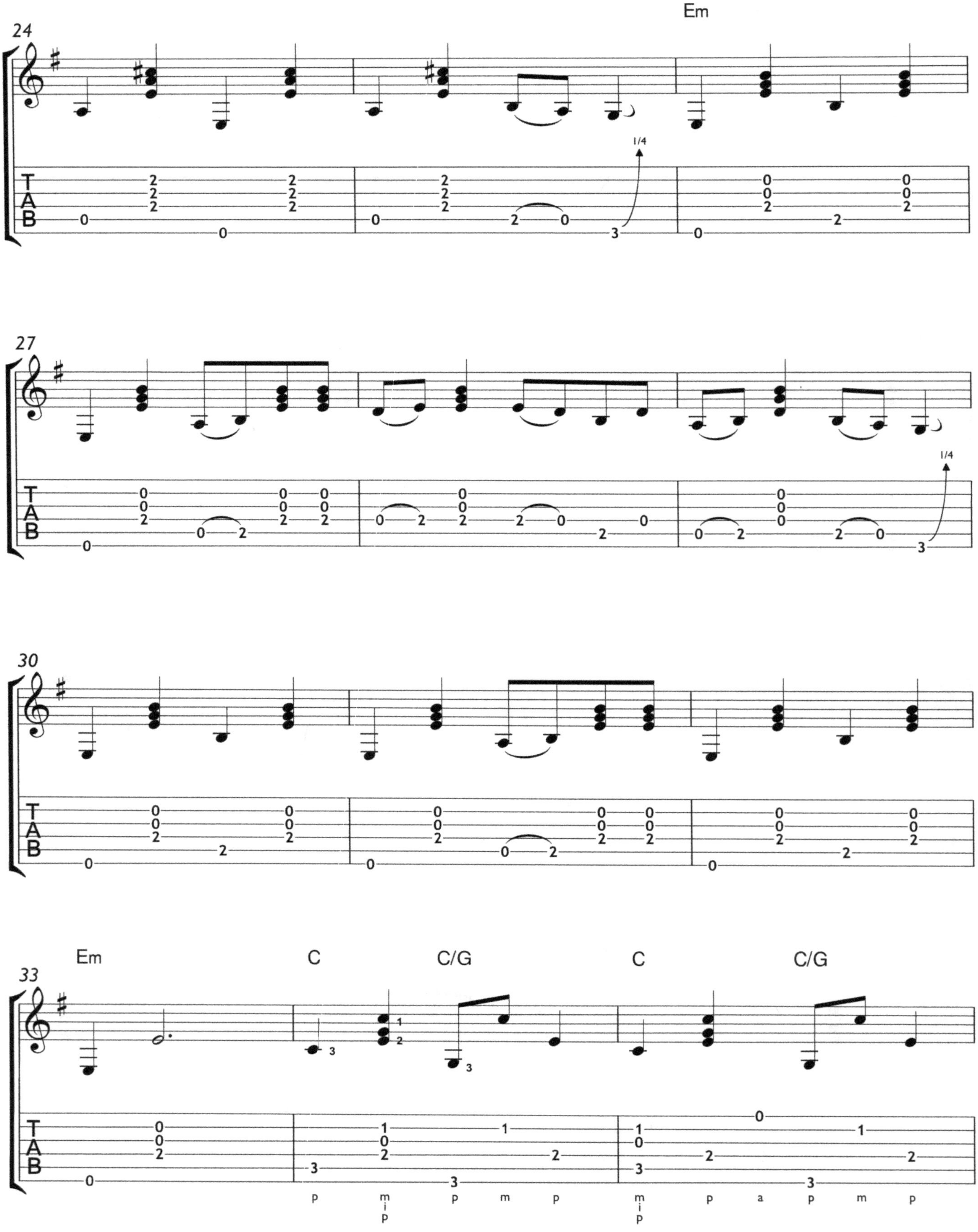
24
Em
1/4
T
A
B
27
1/4
30
33
Em
C
C/G
C
C/G
p m i p p m p m i p p a p m p

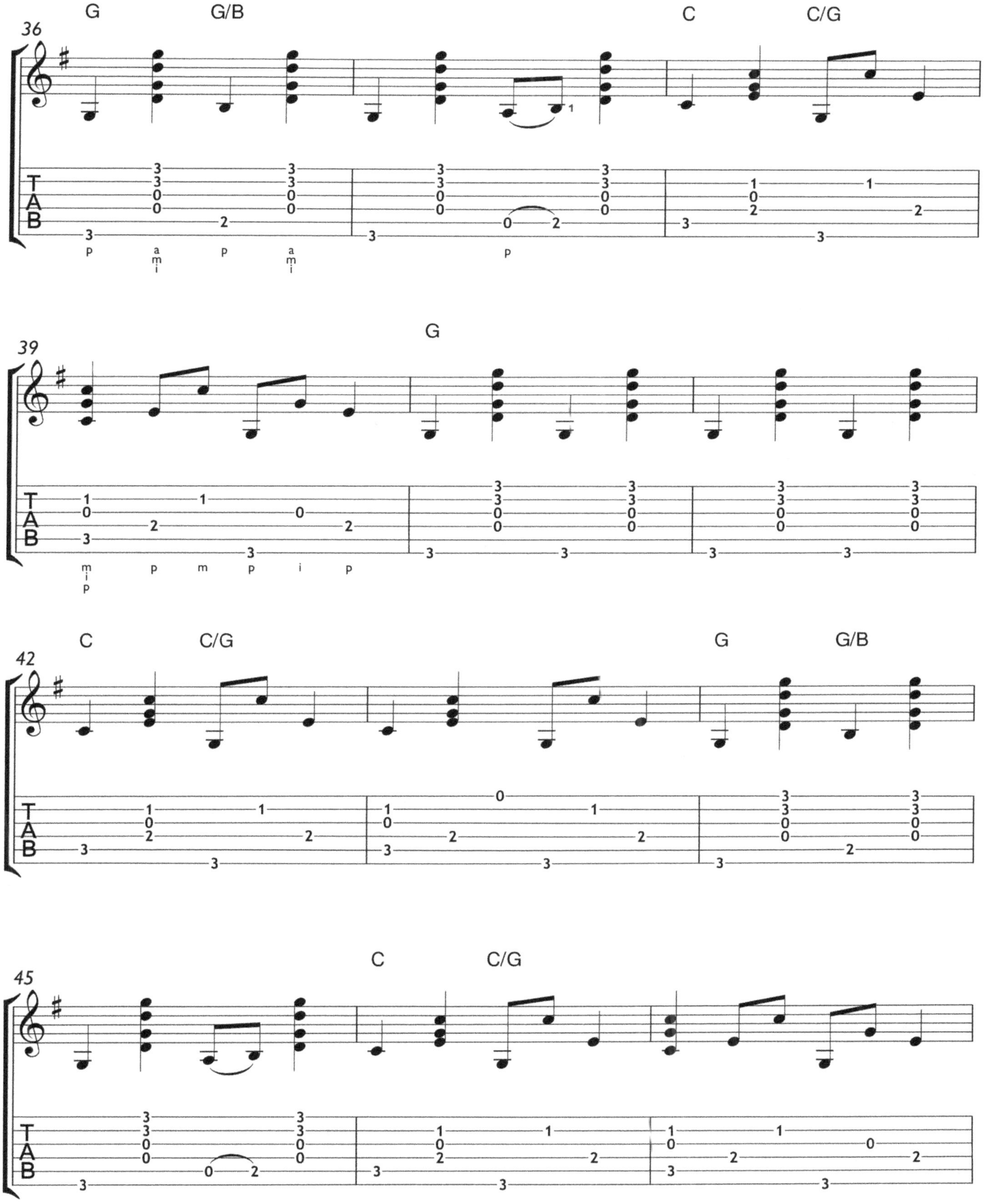
36
G
G/B
C
C/G
T
A
B
p a m i p a m i p
39
G
m i p p m p i p
42
C
C/G
G
G/B
45
C
C/G

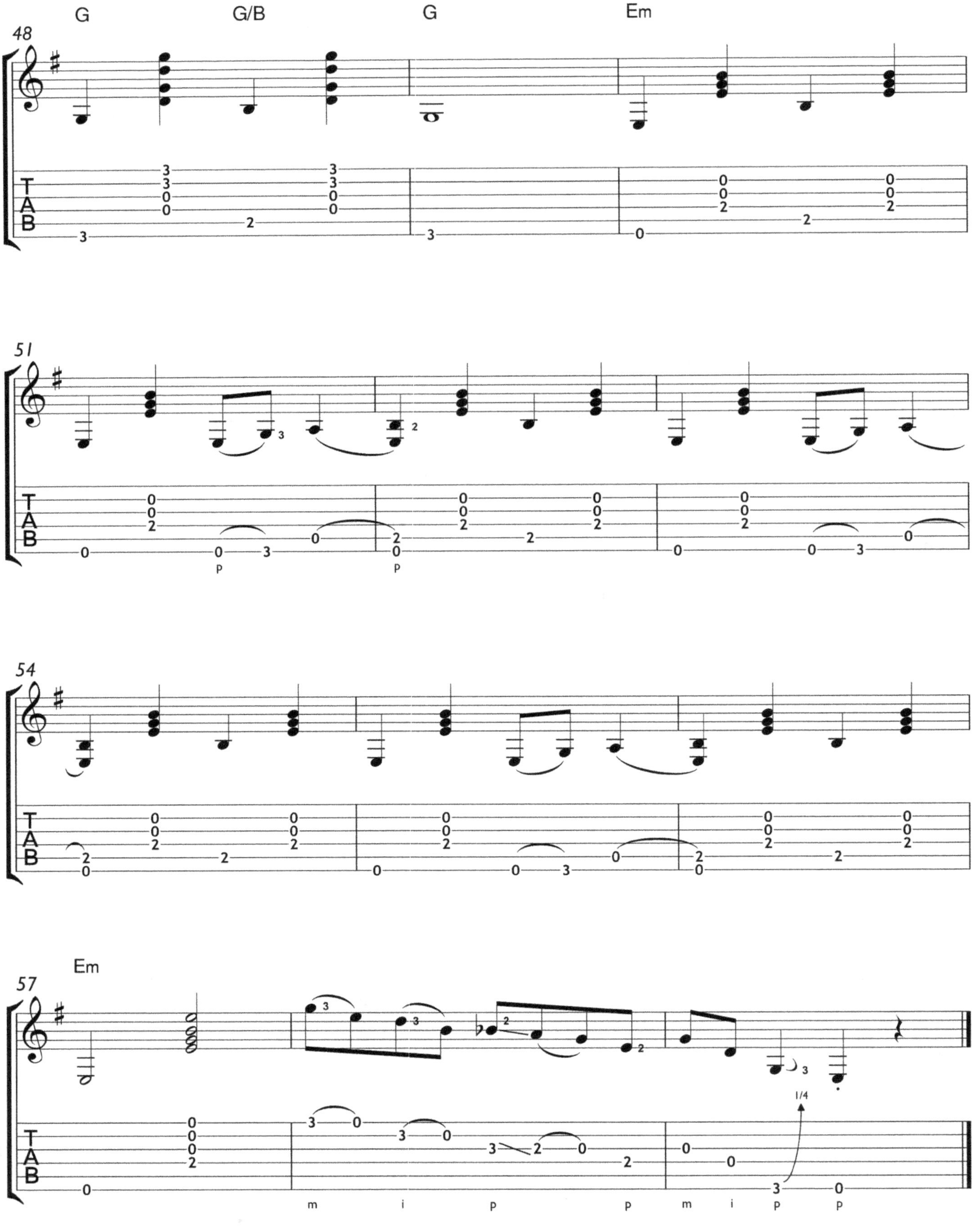
48
G
G/B
G
Em
T
A
B
51
p
p
54
57
Em
1/4
m i p p m i p p

Chapter Four: Bruce Springsteen

Artist Overview

Born in New Jersey on September 23rd, 1949, Bruce Springsteen first developed an interest in music from hearing the superstars of the day – Elvis Presley, Frank Sinatra and The Beatles. As his playing and writing progressed, however, the true Americana sound came to the fore in his acoustic playing, with echoes of Woody Guthrie, Pete Seeger and Bob Dylan to be found within his style. In the early days he used the acoustic guitar in the traditional way, as a device for chordal accompaniment to his vocals. Seminal tracks like *Atlantic City* showcase simple, open chord accompaniment, but as his writing developed and progressed through the years his acoustic parts also become more sophisticated, to include an array of altered tunings and fingerpicked parts that serve to make his guitars parts far more than the "three chord trick" of many renowned acoustic guitarist/ songwriters.

The open tunings lead to chord voicings that go beyond the standard major and minor ideas found in regular tuning. There are sus4, sus2, add9 and add11 chord voicings in his playing. Combine this with his chunky, percussive rhythmic style and you have a powerful approach to acoustic guitar accompaniment that serves to drive a track along – as much a percussive element as a melodic one. This approach to rhythm means the strings take one heck of a beating, as in the style of that other great, Neil Young. It can take some work to get the rhythmic "thwack" in place, so as you go to strike the bass strings with the pick you must quickly apply a picking hand palm mute at the same time. The downward strike with the pick and the damping effect of the palm mute give you that great big rhythm thump.

To get the Springsteen sound into your playing, try using dropped D (string 6 tuned down a tone) and double dropped D tunings (strings 6 and 1 down a tone). This will inevitably pull your writing to the key of D Major, but this is no bad thing – there are some great chord shapes contained within this key – and don't forget that a capo will always take you elsewhere!

Listen and Learn: *Devils and Dust, Atlantic City, The Ghost of Tom Joad, Old Dan Tucker.*

Performance Notes

General Overview

At first, it's tempting to think that the key to Springsteen's powerful rhythm style involves nothing more than brute force and speed. Thankfully, however, this is not the case. Rather, you need to develop a relaxed snap of the wrist in conjunction with a well-timed palm mute to bring out the chunky low end of strings 6 and 5. To practise this, just take the first chord in this study and work on bringing the palm down in the strum, so it quickly bounces off the strings at the bridge at the same moment as the pick strikes the strings. It's a tricky technique to get right, but when you do you will suddenly hear the chords exploding out of the guitar! I've included some suggested strumming patterns to help get you up and running with this one; they are not essential, but try following my suggestions to begin with.

Bar 1 – First make sure you re-tune for this one. We are using double drop D, one of Bruce's favourites! I've written accents above the first few bars to show you which chords need the palm mute/strum approach as outlined. There are two things to bear in mind though: firstly, don't worry too much about hitting the exact notes in the chords as written – to begin with it's more important to focus on the strumming technique and the on\off accent pattern. Secondly, there are some challenges with the rhythms here as they shift from bar to bar, so I'd suggest looping short sections until the accents and rhythms start to become second nature.

Bar 6 – This is a particularly good tuning for this key as it means we can use the low open D (string 6) and the high open D (string 1) on the G chords as well. D is the fifth degree of a G Major chord, so we can use it as the bass note for a heavier sound.

Bar 7 – Here is another common Springsteen voicing. See how this G Major 7 chord sounds different to the G Major in the preceding bar.

Bar 10 – Using those open D strings against an A Major chord also reveals some of the "A" chord shapes that Springsteen likes to use.

Bar 15 – This chord can be a handful but is another common shape in Springsteen's arsenal and sounds great when preceded by a G.

Bar 27 – Using the open strings really serves to thicken up the sound of these A chords and also allows you to move some of the inner voices (in this case the fifth fret on string 4, moving to the fourth fret on the same string) – a very common device in Springsteen's acoustic guitar parts.

Bar 31 – This Dadd4 chord is a great one to commit to memory for any time you are working in this tuning. It is a great alternative to the standard D Major shapes and works particularly well as an intro or ending chord.

Shopping List

Bruce Springsteen usually records with an incredible early 1950s Gibson J45, but given the rigours of the road and his aggressive playing style on stage, you will usually see him playing various Takamine 6 and 12 strings.

♩ = 101

Tuning = DADGBD

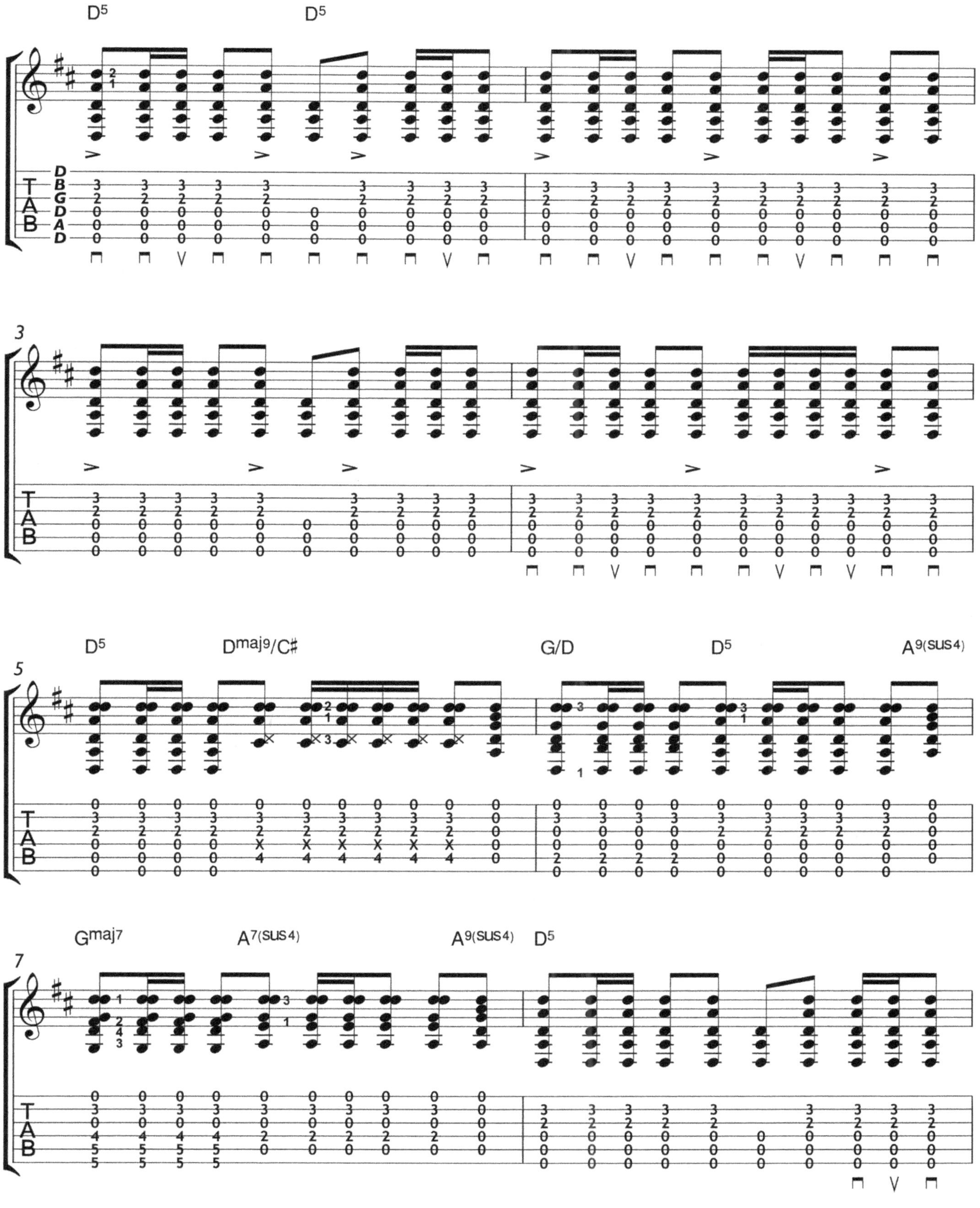

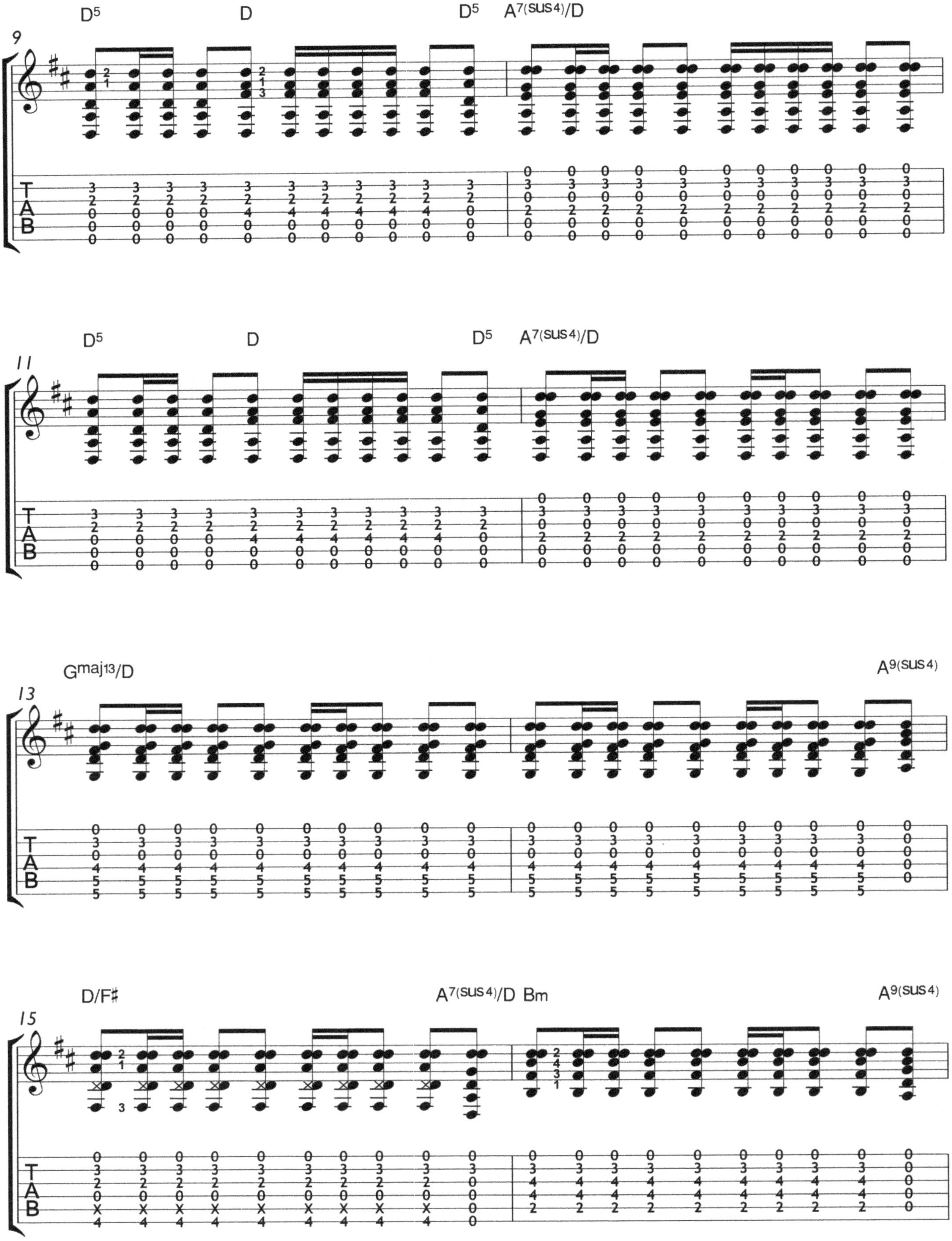
9
D5
D
D5
A7(SUS4)/D
11
D5
D
D5
A7(SUS4)/D
13
Gmaj13/D
A9(SUS4)
15
D/F♯
A7(SUS4)/D
Bm
A9(SUS4)
T
A
B

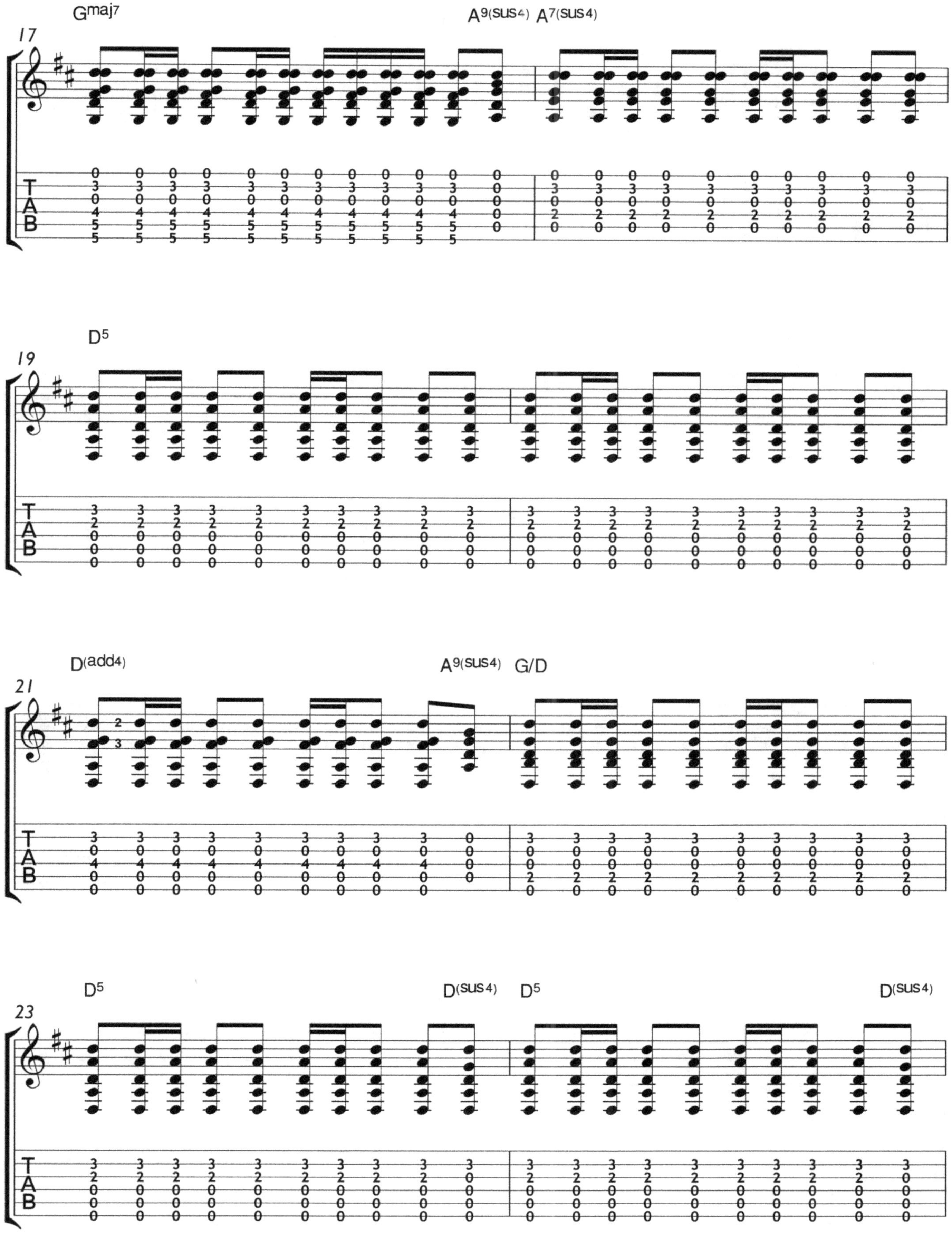

17
Gmaj7
A9(sus4) A7(sus4)
19
D5
21
D(add4)
A9(sus4) G/D
23
D5
D(sus4) D5
D(sus4)

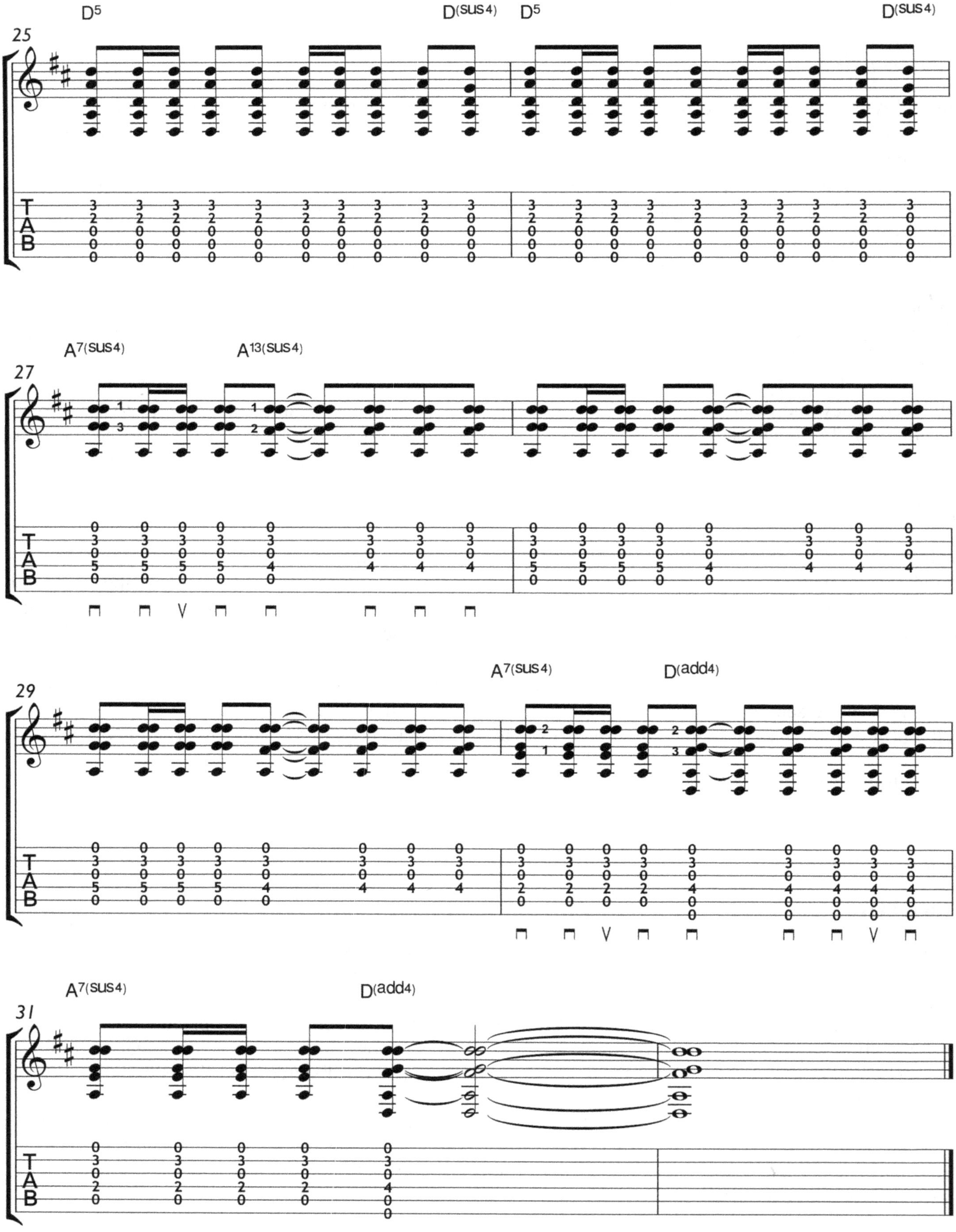
25
D5
D(SUS4)
D5
D(SUS4)
27
A7(SUS4)
A13(SUS4)
29
A7(SUS4)
D(add4)
31
A7(SUS4)
D(add4)

Chapter Five: James Taylor

Artist Overview

James Taylor was born in Boston, USA, on March 12th, 1948. He took up the cello as a child but turned to guitar when he was twelve years old. His early listening and influences consisted mostly of hymns and the guitar playing of Woody Guthrie. Fingerpicking was an early discovery for the young Taylor and he viewed the technique as something that could give him the independence and freedom of a piano player, with the view that the thumb played the role of the pianist's left hand. You can certainly hear this in his playing where basslines interweave with melodic lines and arpeggiated chordal accompaniments. As he entered his teenage years, he discovered Blues and Folk and by age fourteen he was writing his own material.

Taylor moved to New York in the mid-1960s and signed a deal with a small, independent record label. During this time, he developed a serious drug habit which escalated to heroin addiction. Thankfully, he decided that he needed to quit the New York scene and moved to London in 1967. His break came via his friend Danny Kortchmar, who used his connections to get Taylor's demo tape to the fledgling Apple Records and the ears of Paul McCartney and George Harrison. They were hooked by the early versions of *Carolina In My Mind* and *Something In The Way She Moves*. However, Taylor didn't have an instant route to success as he succumbed to heroin addiction once more and committed himself to a psychiatric hospital back in the USA to overcome his issues. Success came after his eventual recovery and the release of his second album, *Sweet Baby James*, in 1970, and the rest is history.

Taylor's wonderful, flowing guitar style emphasizes melodic self-accompaniment and features deftly woven melodic intros that give way to detailed arpeggiated chord lines. In addition, Taylor employs many chords that you won't find in the standard singer-songwriter repertoire, so expect "add" and "sus" chords in his playing – all of which give his writing its unique colour. Given his pianistic approach he also features moving basslines against his chord parts and these can be a challenge to replicate. This, along with the heavily embellished chords, is partly down to his unorthodox fingerings for simple open chords that you would otherwise take for granted. It's not essential to take on board Taylor's fretting hand fingerings in order to play in this style, but it's well worth watching some footage of him perform to see what he does to the standard A and D chord shapes!

Listen and Learn: *Carolina In My Mind, Fire and Rain, You Can Close Your Eyes.*

Performance Notes

General Overview

James Taylor's flowing, heavily embellished fingerpicking style makes him a difficult artist to emulate and this is one of the harder studies in the book. Taylor's music often involves detailed guitar parts, unexpected harmonic twists and turns and melodic guitar intros and breaks. His timing is impeccable, although sometimes he plays with a relaxed, behind the beat feel which can be hard to replicate. This piece is also demanding for the fretting hand, as there will be some new shapes in here for you in addition to a great deal of finger movement within the chords, thanks to his expert embellishments. I'd suggest starting slowly and learning small sections. When you have this piece under your fingers, try using it as a framework for creating your own parts and chord embellishments. For the picking hand you will be able to use the standard *pima* approach where the thumb (*p*) takes care of strings 6, 5 and 4 and the index (*i*), middle (*m*) and ring (*a*) fingers take care of strings 3, 2 and 1 respectively. I've given some suggested fingerings for those occasions where this approach may not be applicable.

Bar 1 – This free-flowing intro is typical of Taylor's writing and showcases his arpeggiated, embellished chords. It's important to remember that if you were playing this unaccompanied as a band intro, your timing would need to be perfect!

Bar 2 – Taylor uses more interesting chords than the standard major and minor shapes and this Em9 is often found in his playing. Adding the 9th (an F#) to the E minor chord results in something called "chord enrichment" and yields a far more interesting sound than the standard E minor.

Bar 3 – Moving out of the open position yields yet more interesting melodic ideas and movement. In this case we are using D and C major triad shapes, favourites of Taylor's when it comes to creating his freestanding intros.

Bar 4 – Having a good knowledge of triad inversions is also key to this style. See how the D major to C major idea is carried on here, but with different inversions of the chords to take us back down the fretboard.

Bar 5 – Here is the first example of how Taylor uses descending basslines in his writing – in this case from the G (fret three, string 6) to an F# (fret two, string 6).

Bar 16 – The embellishment on the A chord is quite tricky here. Remember that Taylor uses an unconventional fingering for his A chord, which makes things a little easier for him, but it is all still accessible with standard fingering.

Bar 17 – Check out the use of the A diminished 7th chord at the end of this bar. This is a "passing chord" used to take use from the A7 to the B minor in the next bar, and is there to facilitate the use of an ascending bassline on string five (from the open string to fret one for the A diminished 7th and fret two for the B minor).

Bar 23 – The C to G chord movement is again smoothed out by bass note movement. The root of the C descends by a semitone to the third (B) of the G chord.

Bars 27-28 – Here is another example of how Taylor will create smooth moving chord progressions by utilizing moving bass notes. In this case we go from a G Major to a G minor simply by moving from the major third of the chord in the bass (B) to the minor third in the bass (Bb).

Shopping List

James Taylor has played many acoustics over the years and recorded his early classics on a Gibson J50. Today he is famous for his James Olsen signature model, a small jumbo-sized instrument. However, you'll need to be feeling very flush if you're going for one as they cost tens of thousands of dollars depending on spec!

♩ = 69

Tuning = EADGBE

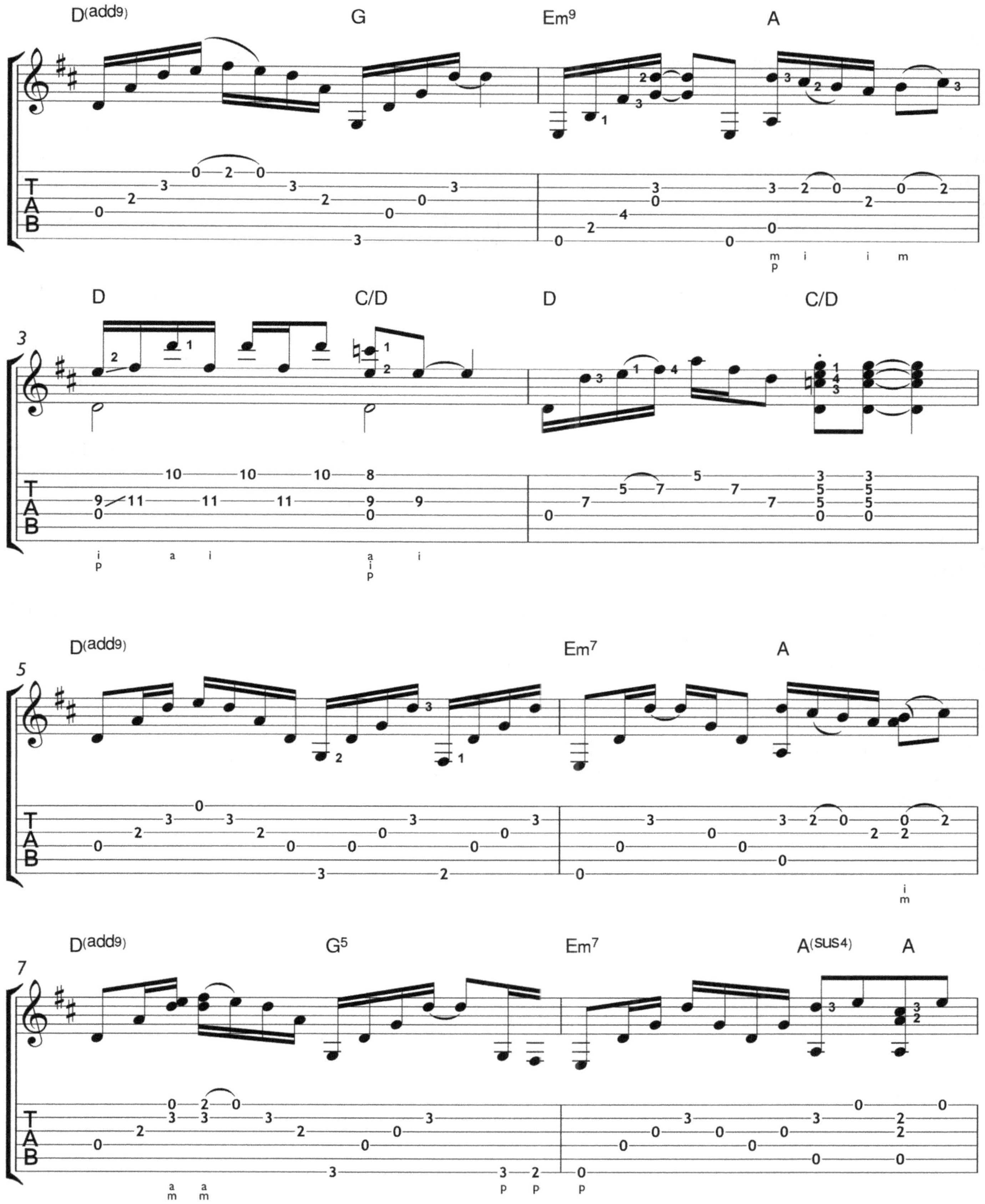

9
D(sus2) C(sus2) G/B D(sus2) C(sus2)
a m i p
11
D C/D G D5
13
C G D5
15
Em9 A7(sus4) Em9 A A(sus2)

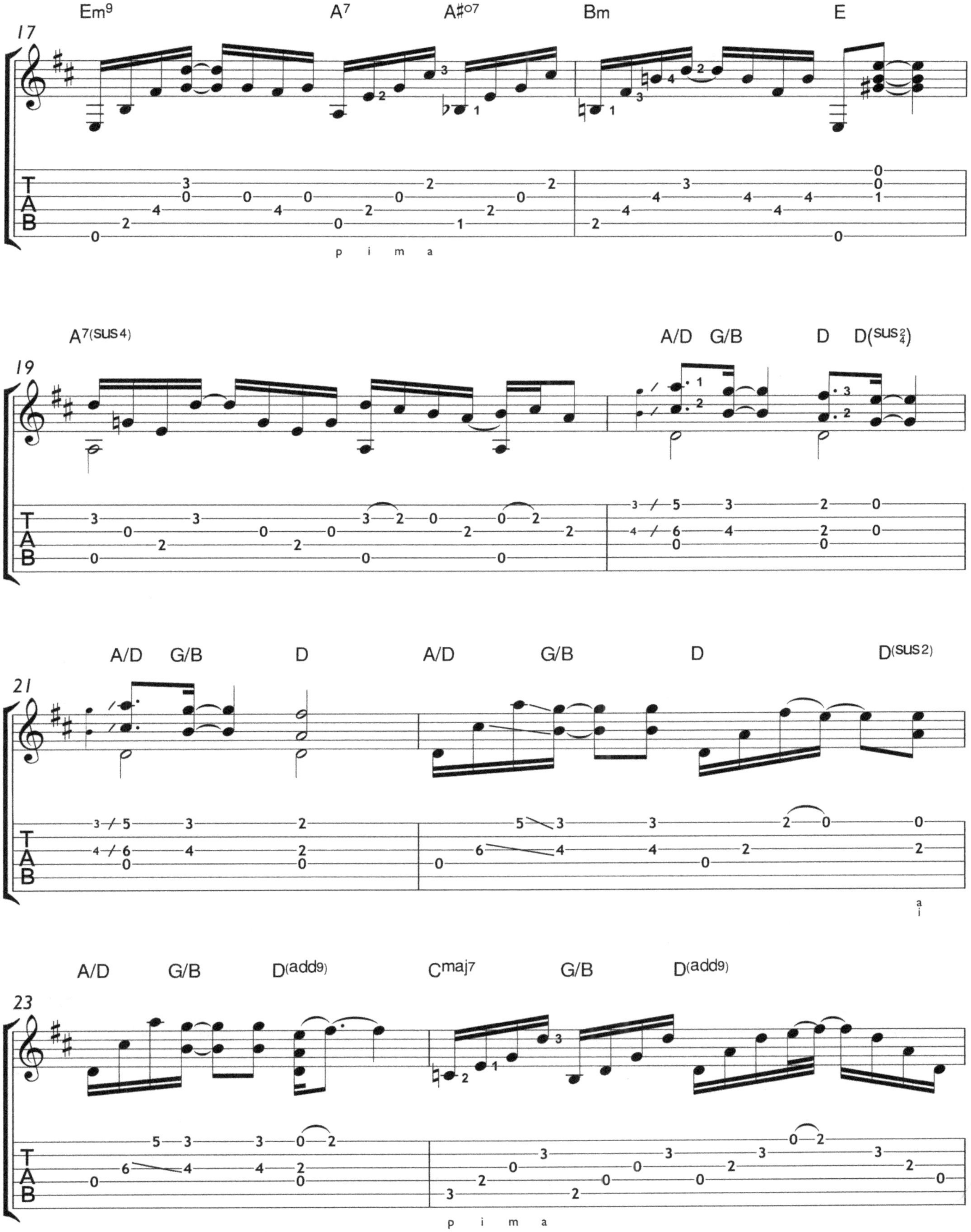
Em9 A7 A#o7 Bm E
17
p i m a
A7(sus4) A/D G/B D D(sus 2/4)
19
A/D G/B D A/D G/B D D(sus2)
21
a i
A/D G/B D(add9) Cmaj7 G/B D(add9)
23
p i m a

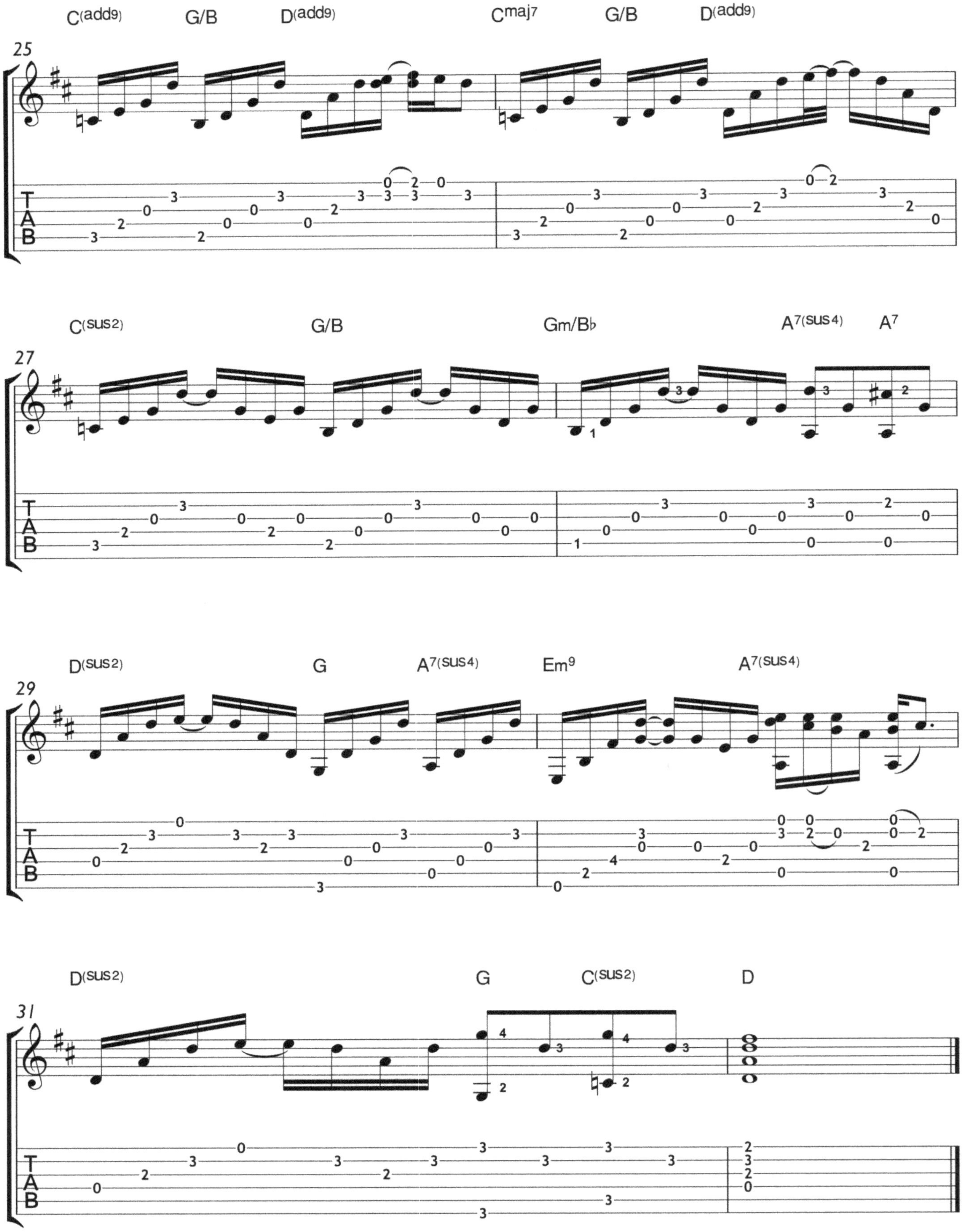
C(add9) G/B D(add9) Cmaj7 G/B D(add9)
25
C(sus2) G/B Gm/B♭ A7(sus4) A7
27
D(sus2) G A7(sus4) Em9 A7(sus4)
29
D(sus2) G C(sus2) D
31

Chapter Six: George Harrison

Artist Overview

Born in Liverpool on February 25, 1943, George Harrison's formative influences were the Rock 'n' Roll legends of his time, principally Buddy Holly and Little Richard. However, like most guitarists, he was also drawn to the more "technical" players of the era and developed an interest in Rockabilly legend Carl Perkins, Gypsy Jazz genius Django Reinhardt and bluesman Big Bill Broonzy. With such a diverse palette of influences, it's no surprise that he became the predominantly "lead" guitarist in The Beatles. Throughout his solo career you can hear elements of all these players, not least in his unexpected chord progressions where jazz influenced diminished seventh chords could suddenly appear when least expected.

Arguably the most guitar-focused musician of The Beatles, George's acoustic playing is full of character and in this study we'll see how unexpected chords can really bring a piece to life. In this study you'll encounter some unusual chord moves that will serve as a great exercise for the fretting hand. The picking hand will focus on tight, rhythmic strumming and clean arpeggiated chords. If the diminished seventh chords are new to you, try playing them on their own to begin with, as both the sound and fingering may sound a little alien. These tense, dissonant chords don't often find their way into Pop/Rock writing, but George's genius was in using them as transition points between the more obvious major and minor chord progressions. You'll also come across a variety of "sus" chords here, as well as a common, though challenging, way of playing an Fmaj7 chord where the fretting hand thumb is employed over the top of the neck – a common device for guitar players in the 1950s, 60s and beyond.

Listen and Learn: *Isn't It a Pity, While My Guitar Gently Weeps, The Ballad of Sir Frankie Crisp, Here Comes the Sun.*

Performance Notes

General Overview

George's vocabulary makes him an interesting and sophisticated study. Although we are focusing on a mostly strummed/acoustic rhythm guitar part in this track, it's the variety of chord voicings within the progression and the bass note/chord strumming pattern which helps the acoustic part add "glue" to the track. Although you could lightly strum and pick this with the picking hand fingers, I'd use a plectrum, something medium-light so you can get the required attack without having the acoustic dominate the track. Timing shouldn't be too much of an issue with this track, so the biggest challenge is probably for the fretting hand to get used to the diminished seventh chord shapes and the general chordal movement around the fretboard.

Bar 1 – Although not exclusive to George Harrison's guitar style, this bass/chord strumming approach is a great thing to have in your technique arsenal. In effect, it mimics the bass/chord or left/right hand technique of a piano player. Downstrokes can be used all the way here to keep a driving, even rhythm in place.

Bar 3 – Our first "unexpected" chord is a C# diminished seventh that really adds some colour to the sound and takes us away from the standard, predictable chord progressions so common to pop music of this era.

Bar 7 – Here is another diminished seventh chord to catch the ear. Note that this shape can be moved around the fretboard in minor thirds (three semitones) but always contains the same notes, so an E diminished seventh chord is also a C# diminished seventh, G diminished seventh and Bb diminished seventh. You can see the effect of moving this chord up in bar 12.

Bar 16 – There is a very Beatles-esque pause on this D9 (with no 3rd) chord!

Bar 18 – Guitarists from the 1950s and 1960s eras would play this Fmaj7 voicing by hooking the fretting hand thumb over the top of the neck to fret the first fret of string 6. It's a great way of keeping the open first string clear to achieve that Fmaj7 sound. You'll hear it from players from other genres too and Chet Atkins used this shape a lot.

Bar 23 – Another songwriting trick used by George but certainly not exclusive to him – the IV Major chord (C) briefly changes to a dominant (C7) before reverting to the I chord (G).

Shopping List

You'll generally see footage of George with a Gibson J160E or Gibson SJ200 acoustic, both during his time with The Beatles and the subsequent solo years.

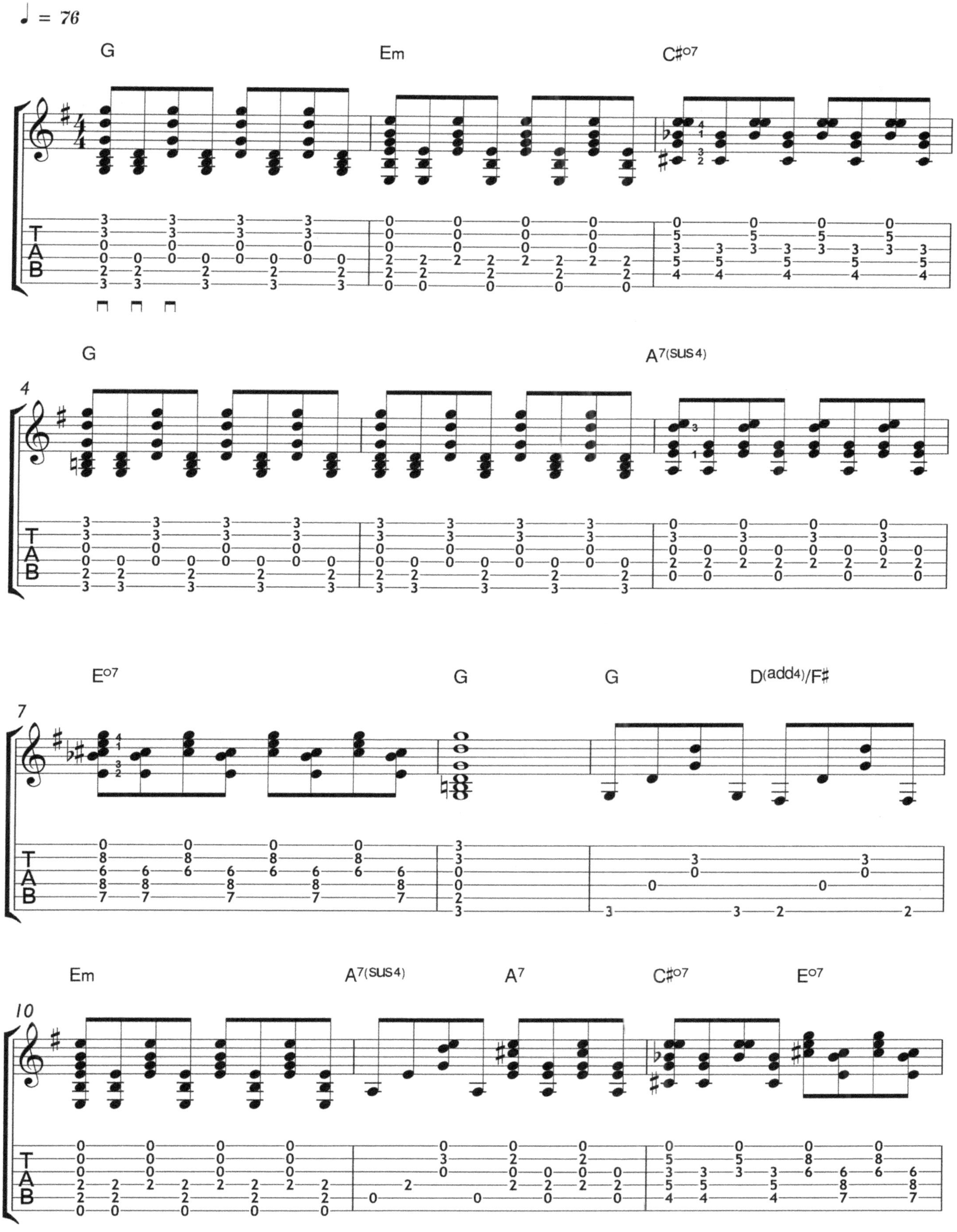
♩ = 76
G
Em
C♯o7
4
G
A7(sus4)
7
Eo7
G
G
D(add4)/F♯
10
Em
A7(sus4)
A7
C♯o7
Eo7

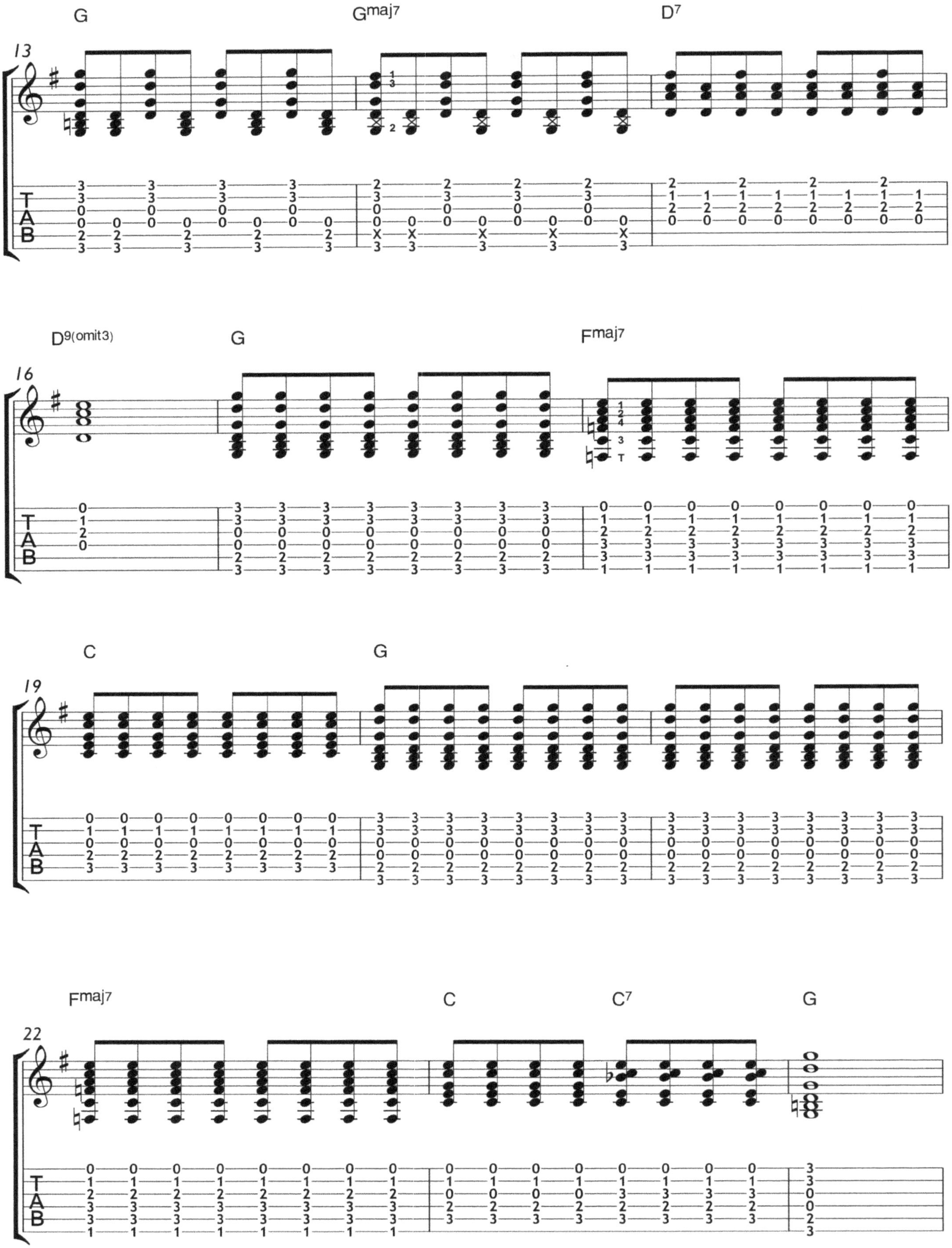
G
Gmaj7
D7
13
D9(omit3)
G
Fmaj7
16
C
G
19
Fmaj7
C
C7
G
22

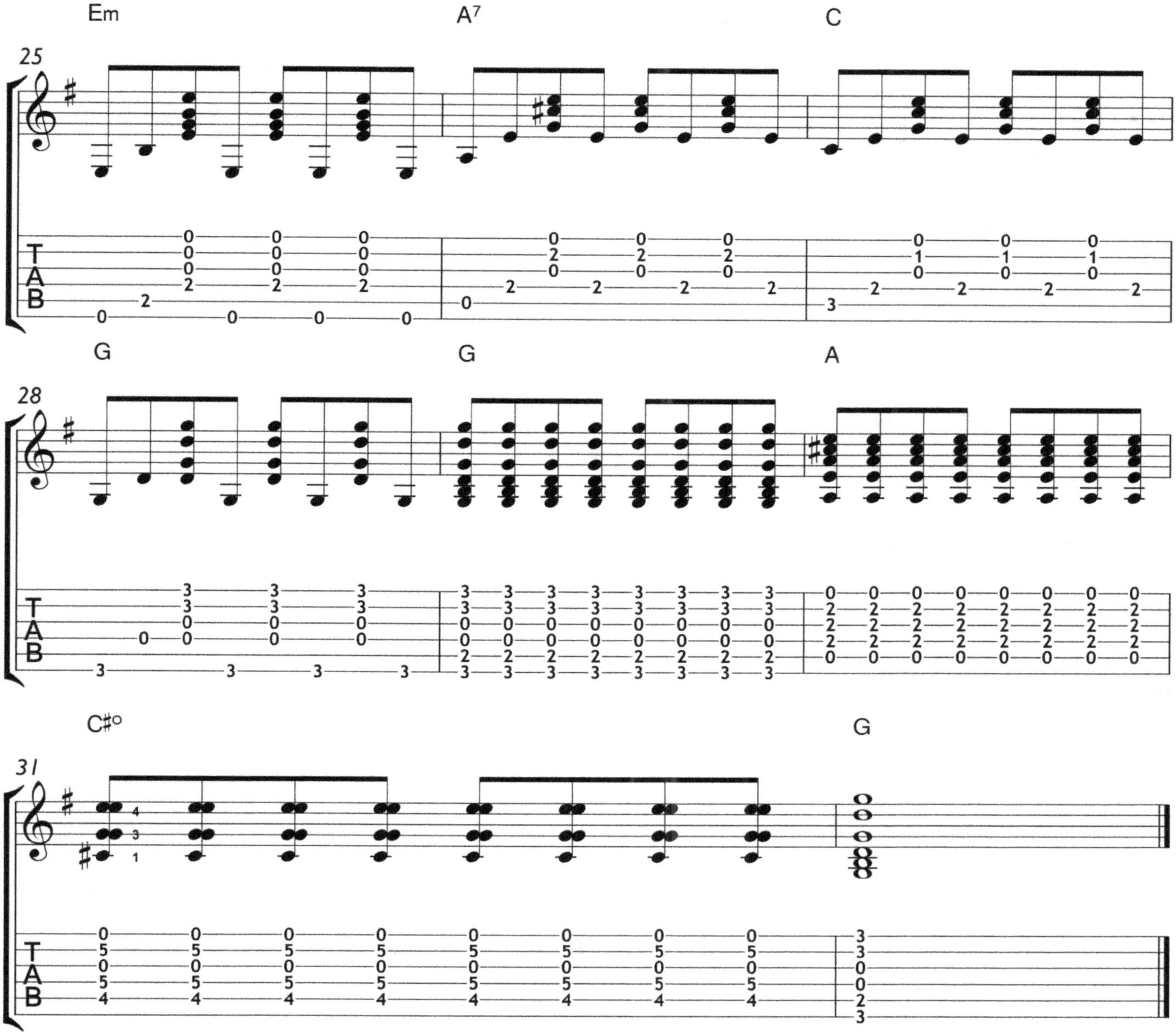
Em
A7
C
25
TAB
G
G
A
28
TAB
C♯o
G
31
TAB

Chapter Seven: Neil Young

Artist Overview

Born in Toronto on November 12, 1945, Neil Young's formative musical influences came from the worlds of Rock 'n' Roll, Rockabilly, Country, Doo-wop and Rhythm and Blues. His childhood idol was Elvis Presley, but he was also drawn to the sounds of Hank Marvin, Link Wray, Roy Orbison and many others. At the heart of his playing is that classic American sound: a wistful, Country-Folk sound that conjures up evocative pastoral images. He is, however, a wildly diverse player and can be found in several different contexts, from fuzz driven electric guitar grunge to the Country-Folk tinged sound of albums like *After the Goldrush* and *Harvest*. Both a fingerpicker and a strummer like Springsteen, you'll hear him use altered tunings and a heavy, percussive downstroke when strumming to get those big, chunky rhythm parts in place.

This study focuses on Young's chordal rhythm playing as heard on the *Harvest* album. His lovely, relaxed timing is an essential element to master, so aim for a lazy, swing feel throughout here. Also important is the dynamic range on his strumming hand from light to heavy, so make sure you explore the widest possible scope when strumming through this one. His playing also provides a great lesson in how using open strings can act as a hinge that keeps a chord sequence together, and in this lesson we'll focus on the open first string as such a cohesive device. The softer chord sounds are, in part, derived by using chords like Major 6ths that help produce that rich, pastoral sound. A bit less obvious than simple major chords they are well worth studying and getting into your playing and writing. Notice also how we move shapes up and down strings 1, 2 and 3 but keep the 6th, 5th and 4th strings open to provide some real low-end weight.

Listen and Learn: *Harvest Moon, Needle and The Damage Done, The Old Laughing Lady.*

Performance Notes

General Overview

Neil Young is both a fingerpicker and strummer, but in this study we will look at his relaxed, slightly swung strumming style. You can strum this with just the fingers or a pick. If going with the latter, I'd recommend a thin-medium pick to keep the sound and volume balanced. The chordal element of Young's guitar playing is also an essential element of what makes it unique. Whether by accident or design, he has a masterful ear when it comes to voicing chords on the acoustic guitar, always choosing those that sound rich and colourful. In many ways his use of major sixths and sevenths helps characterize the calm pastoral nature of his acoustic Country-Folk playing. I've indicated suggested down and upstrokes for the strumming patterns; these are not essential to follow but you may find they help – ending a bar with a quaver and an upstroke puts you in place for a strong downstroke at the start of the next bar.

Bar 1 – There are two key elements before we get going: firstly, the dropped D tuning (string 6 down a tone) and secondly the light swing feel. Make sure you have these in place before progressing! The swing feel can be tricky to execute, but listen to the audio track and you'll get the idea.

Bar 3 – Think "dynamics" all the way. The opening note (open 6th string) can be played with a strong downstroke and preferably with some palm muting, as with the Springsteen study. Try following this with a lighter touch on the next chord, the D6/9.

Bar 6 – By now you should have heard some of the inner voices (fretted notes) moving within these chords – a hallmark of Young's acoustic guitar writing which creates a more interesting sound than using a single chord for each part of the progression.

Bar 8 – Often Young uses big sounding open strings with just two or three fretted notes, which create a contrast to the big low end, with melodic content up on strings 3, 2 and 1.

Bar 17 – Moving the inner voices higher up the neck creates even more of a contrast between the low end, provided by the open 6th, 5th and 4th strings, and the higher notes on strings 3, 2 and 1. In fact, it almost creates the illusion of two guitars playing at once and allows for interesting harmonic movement.

Bar 34 – The contrast between big, open chords and just the low open bass strings (6 and 5) is a great device. Try moving both around within the bar and also try the open bass strings with and without the palm muting approach.

Shopping List

Neil Young is a big fan of the Martin D-18 and generally for this style, a larger dreadnought style guitar is preferable. It will give you the big low-end thump you are looking for.

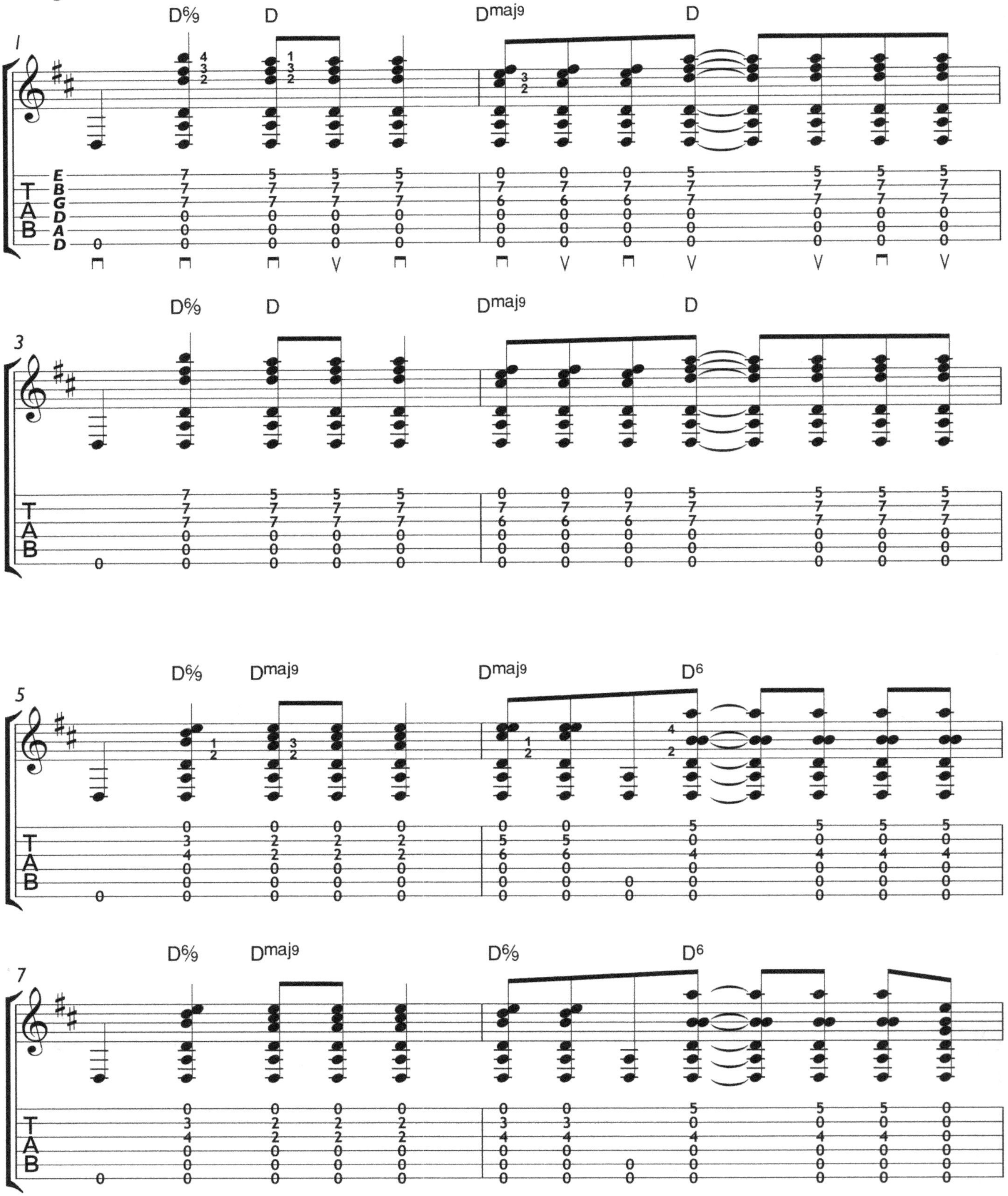

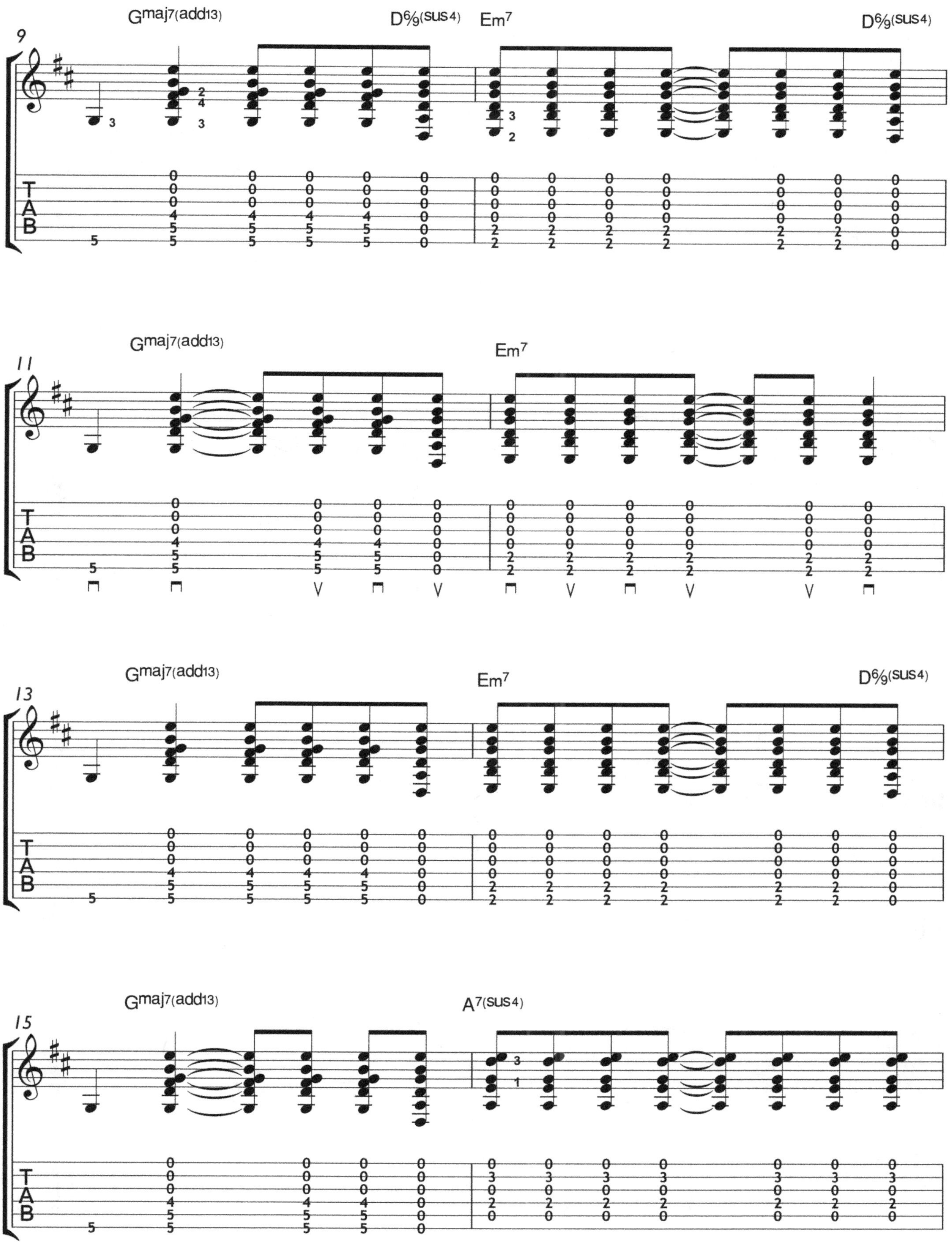
9
Gmaj7(add13)
D6/9(sus4)
Em7
D6/9(sus4)
11
Gmaj7(add13)
Em7
13
Gmaj7(add13)
Em7
D6/9(sus4)
15
Gmaj7(add13)
A7(sus4)
TAB

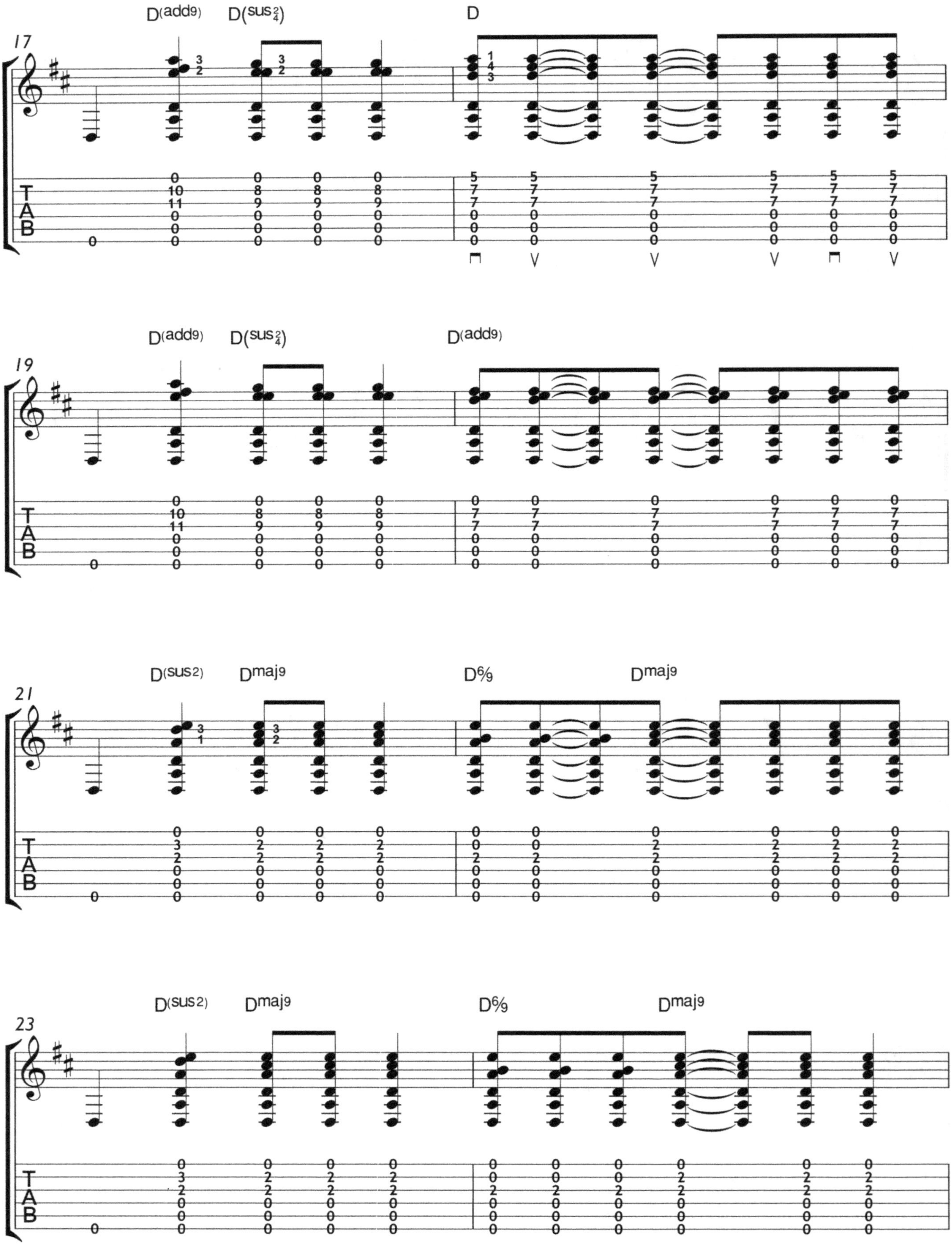
17
D(add9)
D(sus2/4)
D
19
D(add9)
D(sus2/4)
D(add9)
21
D(sus2)
Dmaj9
D6/9
Dmaj9
23
D(sus2)
Dmaj9
D6/9
Dmaj9
TAB

25
A7(SUS4)
A6
TAB
27
A7(SUS4)
A7
TAB
29
A7(SUS4)
A6
TAB
31
A7(SUS4)
A7
TAB

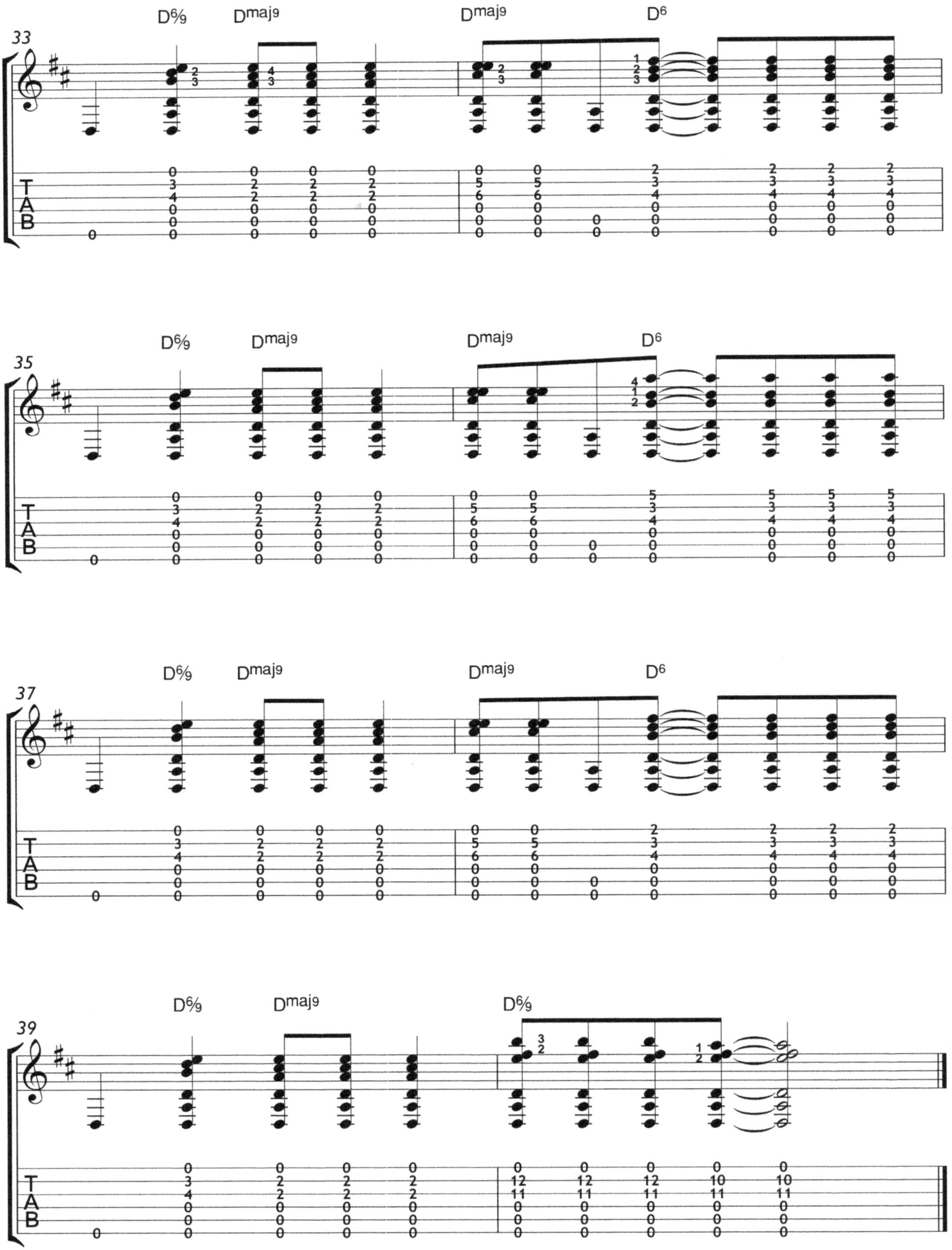
33
D6/9
Dmaj9
Dmaj9
D6
TAB
35
D6/9
Dmaj9
Dmaj9
D6
TAB
37
D6/9
Dmaj9
Dmaj9
D6
TAB
39
D6/9
Dmaj9
D6/9
TAB

Chapter Eight: Tracy Chapman

Artist Overview

Born on March 30th, 1964, in Cleveland, Ohio, Tracy Chapman started her musical life at age three when her mother bought her a ukulele. Five years later she took up guitar and started writing her first songs. As she became older, Chapman became highly politicized and socially aware, not least thanks to the juxtapositions in her own life: going from growing up in a poor neighbourhood to winning a scholarship to an exclusive boarding school. Although she is often labelled a Folk singer or "protest singer" Chapman prefers to draw from a bigger musical picture, rather than fall back on the influence of classic protest singers like Bob Dylan and Joan Baez. Her early influences came from the Country genre and included artists like Charley Pride, Dolly Parton, Glen Campbell and legendary Country guitarist Buck Owens. Alongside these influences she grew up listening to Soul, Gospel and Jazz but, interestingly, not Folk!

Singing within her family unit was her main musical expression to begin with, which she did from a very young age. Then, as with many performers of her generation, she began performing on the coffee house circuit and busking while at university. She got her big break via a fellow student whose father worked in music publishing. After an introduction and audition he helped her broker a deal with Elektra Records that led to her debut album, *Tracy Chapman*, being released in 1988. This album contains the tracks that made her a star, *Fast Car* and *Talkin' 'Bout a Revolution* amongst them. The opportunity to perform *Fast Car* at the Nelson Mandela Birthday Tribute concert on June 11, 1988, gave her sudden exposure to a worldwide audience and this resulted in *Fast Car* reaching the Top 10 of the American Billboard 100.

Chapman's guitar style is not difficult to master, but she is a great example of how an acoustic guitar part can fit into a track from several perspectives. She uses simple fingerpicking parts from the typical Folk style to bolster the vocals, or basic strumming patterns to fill out the rhythm section. But she also uses "thin" parts to create more melodic movement. Listen to *Fast Car* and you will hear her using intervals of 10ths which create a more melodic part than simply arpeggiating a chord (a 10th chord consists of the root note and the third shifted up an octave). One of the most famous examples of this type of writing is Paul McCartney's *Blackbird* and it's possible that this influenced Chapman when writing her song. Although there are no major challenges in this study, as ever focus on getting your timing tight and the parts accurate and clean throughout.

Listen and Learn: *Fast Car, Talkin' 'Bout a Revolution, Baby Can I Hold You Tonight*.

Performance Notes

This study is a good exercise in both rhythmic, clean fingerpicking and strumming. The main 'verse' contains some melodic movement within the chords so will require all the picking hand fingers to sound the notes with an even dynamic – ensure that the low bass notes aren't louder than the top melody line as this is the hook that will draw a listener in. A standard 'pima' picking hand approach will work well for the fingerpicked sections.

General Overview

Bar 1 – This study can be played entirely with the fingers or with a combination of pick and fingers. You can either use the picking hand fingers in conjunction with the pick (hybrid picking) or tuck the pick in the fingers or palm and take it out when you get to the strumming sections. This first bar shows how Chapman will take a standard chord shape and employ melodic movement within it to create a more memorable hook-based part.

Bar 2 – Using "thin" chords is another typical Chapman device, like those found in McCartney's *Blackbird*. This makes it easier to create a cohesive sense of movement: the G chord only features the third (B) on the bass and fifth (D) on the top and moves smoothly to the bass root of the C chord (C) and the third of that chord (E).

Bar 6 – As in bar 2, here is another example of how using the wide intervals creates more of a hook as opposed to moving large, full-voiced chords around.

Bar 9 – Another classic device is simply to change the bass note of a chord or sequence to produce a new tonality. Instead of a C Major sound, here we get A minor just by changing the bass note. The top line (or riff idea) stays the same, but the effect is wholly different.

Bar 17 – We now change to the strumming section. If you are finger picking then brush up and down the strings with the nails of your index, middle and ring fingers. If you have a pick tucked in the palm or between the fingers, now is the time to use it! Notice how the G note on the top of the C chord remains in place when we move to the G chord in the next bar. This device is known as a "common tone" – a note that belongs to both chords – and gives a smooth sense of movement from the C to G chords. Look out for the shifting rhythms in this section.

Bar 19 – Add9 chords like the Cadd9 used here are great alternatives to standard Major chords. The 9th note is a tone above the root note, shifted up an octave. The root is C, so here we add a D note to the chord.

Bar 33 – Here is a more detailed example of the wide interval approach in Chapman's playing. Note how this effectively creates a melody with a bassline underneath and the open 3rd string (G) acts as a hinge between each part of this section.

Shopping List

Chapman is in love with her 1967 Martin D35, but given the age and fragility of that instrument on the road she often travels and performs with a Martin Backpacker and a Taylor Baby – both small bodied travel guitars. She also uses a parlour-sized acoustic built by Canadian luthier Judy Threet and a Santa Cruz P.

♩ = 104

Tuning = EADGBE

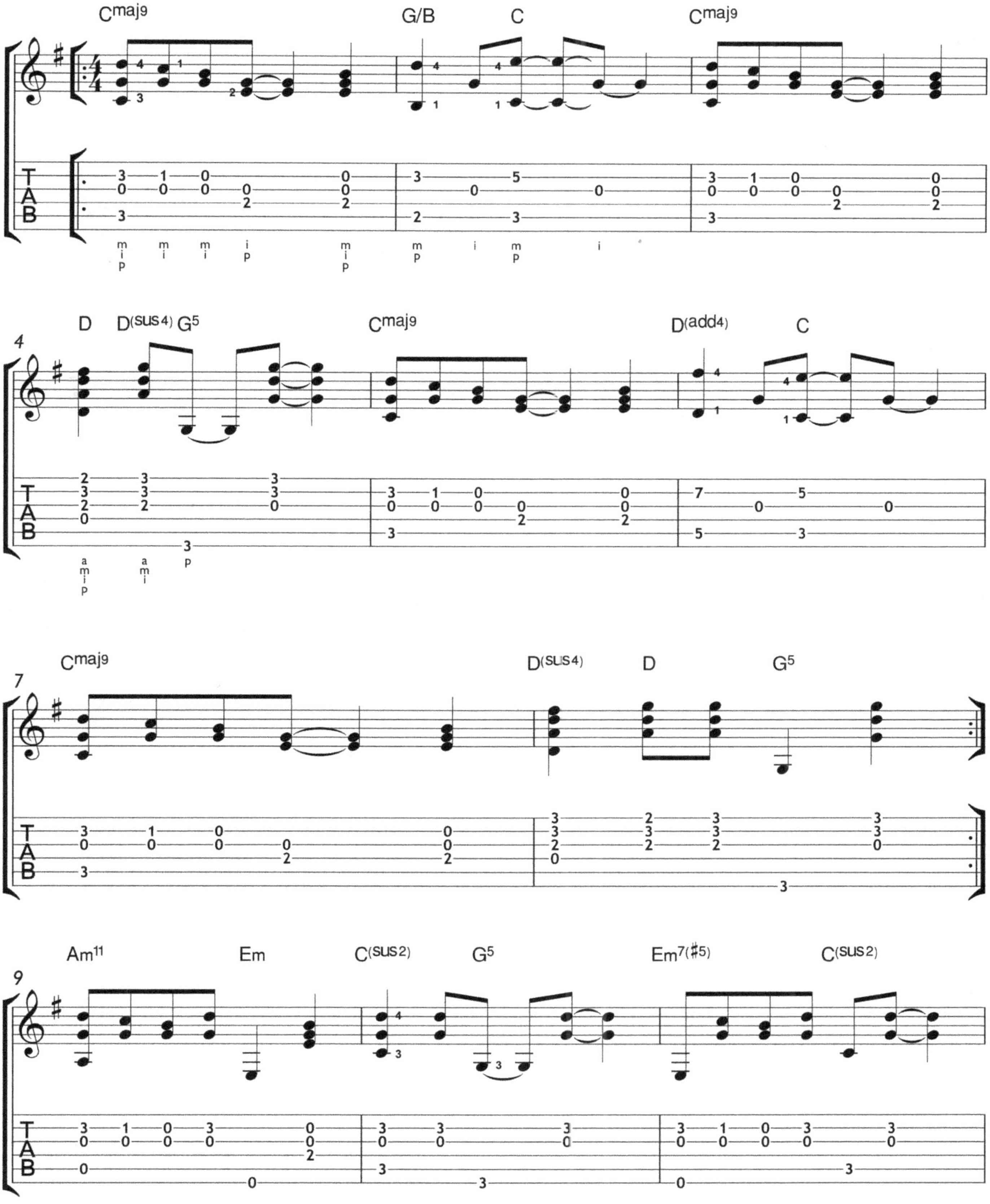

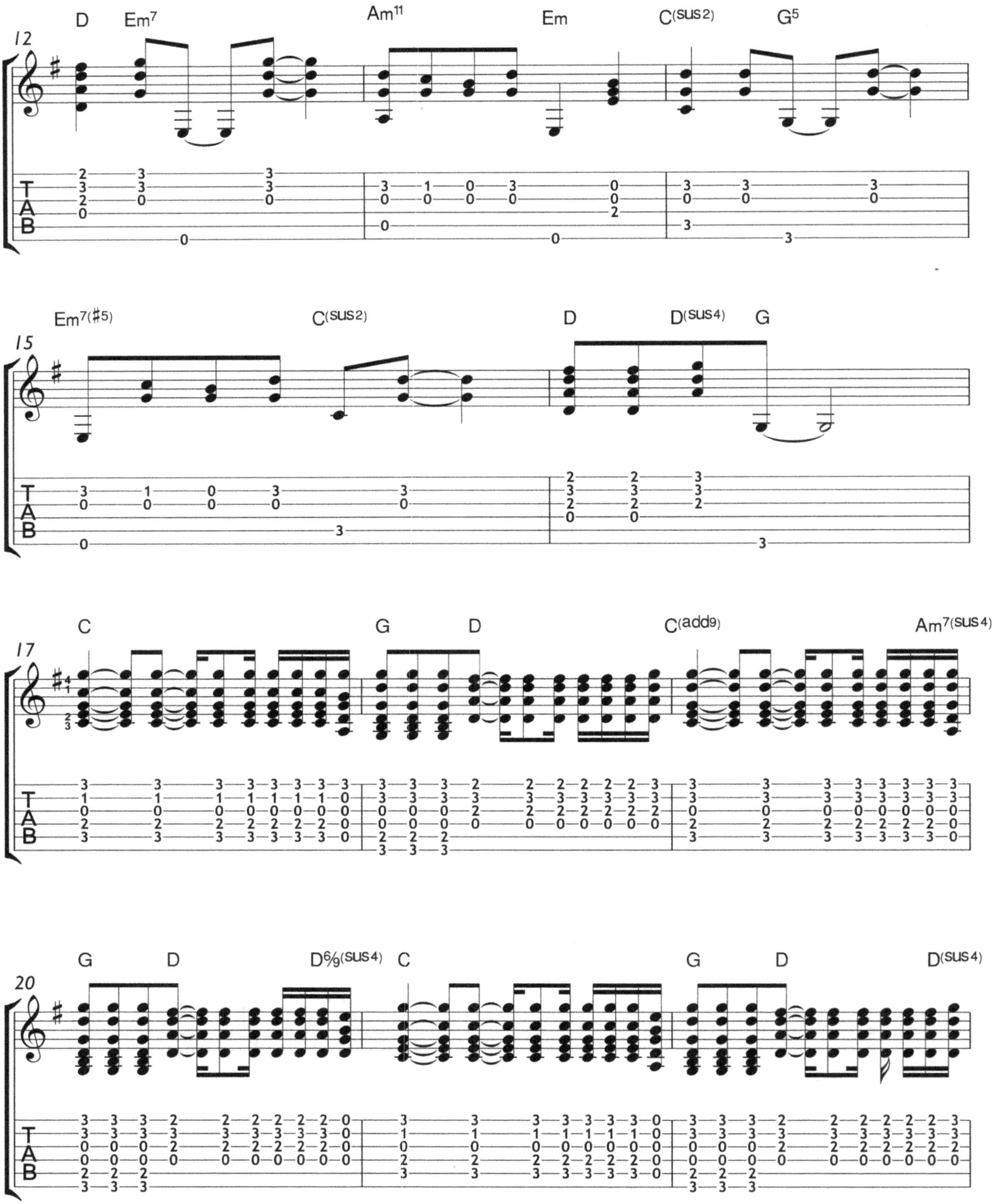
12
D
Em7
Am11
Em
C(sus2)
G5
15
Em7(♯5)
C(sus2)
D
D(sus4)
G
17
C
G
D
C(add9)
Am7(sus4)
20
G
D
D6/9(sus4)
C
G
D
D(sus4)
TAB

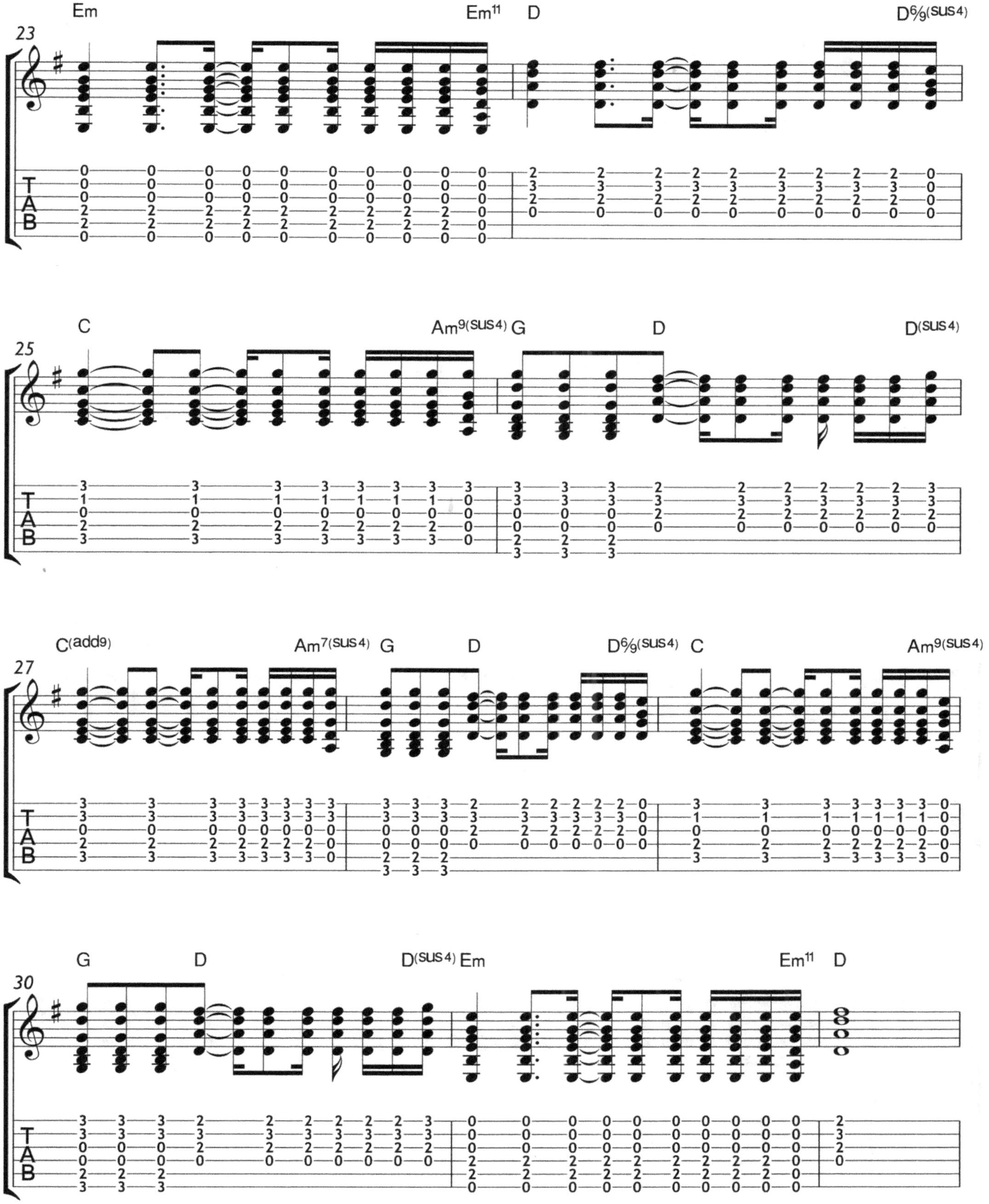
Em
Em11
D
D6/9(sus4)
23
C
Am9(sus4)
G
D
D(sus4)
25
C(add9)
Am7(sus4)
G
D
D6/9(sus4)
C
Am9(sus4)
27
G
D
D(sus4)
Em
Em11
D
30
TAB

33
Em G D(add4) C Em G
36
D(add4) C Em G D(add4) C
39
Em G G/B C G(add4)
42
D D(sus4) Em Cmaj9 G5 D G
TAB

Chapter Nine: John Mayer

Artist Overview

John Mayer was born on October 16th, 1977, in Bridgeport, Connecticut. His earliest and biggest influences were electric bluesmen Stevie Ray Vaughan, Buddy Guy and the three Kings – BB, Freddie and Albert – amongst others. A songwriter from the age of 17, it was inevitable that the acoustic guitar would come calling and during his brief tenure at the Berklee College of Music in Boston during 1997 he became a regular fixture, performing at the city's many coffee shops. His debut EP, *Inside Wants Out* features some spectacular acoustic playing influenced in large part by San Francisco fingerstyle Jazz genius Charlie Hunter. Mayer's track *Neon* is a tip of the hat to Hunter's indomitable self-accompaniment style.

Mayer's acoustic writing is complex. He has a huge chord vocabulary which he uses to add great colour to his writing and his fingerstyle technique is formidable. His early releases like *Room For Squares* and *Heavier Things* showcase some superb Pop/Rock acoustic guitar writing, but latterly his acoustic sound has become more influenced by the classic Americana/Country sound: Neil Young, Joni Mitchell, James Taylor, Crosby Stills and Nash, Bob Dylan and Jorma Kaukonen loom large in his style now.

Mayer's parts on his recent albums like *Born and Raised* and *Paradise Valley* are fantastic groove-based, melodic ideas and his consistent timing is always in evidence with his right hand. In addition, he is a master at embellishing simple chord progressions so that they become so much more. This is in evidence in his electric playing via his Jimi Hendrix and Stevie Ray Vaughan influences, but on acoustic he approaches it from the Americana/Country perspective – you'll find open chords with melodic embellishments and extensions that just flow through a track so perfectly.

Listen and Learn: *Neon, Queen of California, Stop This Train.*

Performance Notes

Fingerstyle guitar has always been at the forefront of John Mayer's playing and writing and in his early days he used a complex bass accompaniment style heavily influenced by Jazz guitarist Charlie Hunter. Over recent years his fingerstyle playing has simplified a little and currently he seems to spend more time examining the styles and techniques of the classic acoustic Folk/Americana players from the 1950s and 1960s. Although you could perform this piece with the standard *pima* picking hand patterns, I've also suggested some alternate fingerings which remove the "a" finger from the equation. Try these and you may feel things flow more naturally for the picking hand in this context.

General Overview

Bar 1 – Mayer often uses a capo when accompanying his voice, so I've used a capo on fret 4 here to put the piece in the key of B Major. You can play this without a capo (in which case you'll be in the key of G Major), but you'll need it if you want to play along with the backing track. Notice how the capo sweetens and brightens the sound of parts like this, which can sometimes sound muddy played in open position. The bass note at the start of beat one should be plucked with the picking hand thumb. The chord immediately following can be plucked with the index, middle and ring fingers, but you can also brush down the strings with the nails of the same fingers.

Bar 2 – Watch out for the fleet run at the end of this bar. This bluegrass-tinged lick hints at the classic American Folk sound that has found its way into Mayer's playing over the years. Try using my suggested picking hand fingerings for this piece as it is rather more detailed than some of the others in this book.

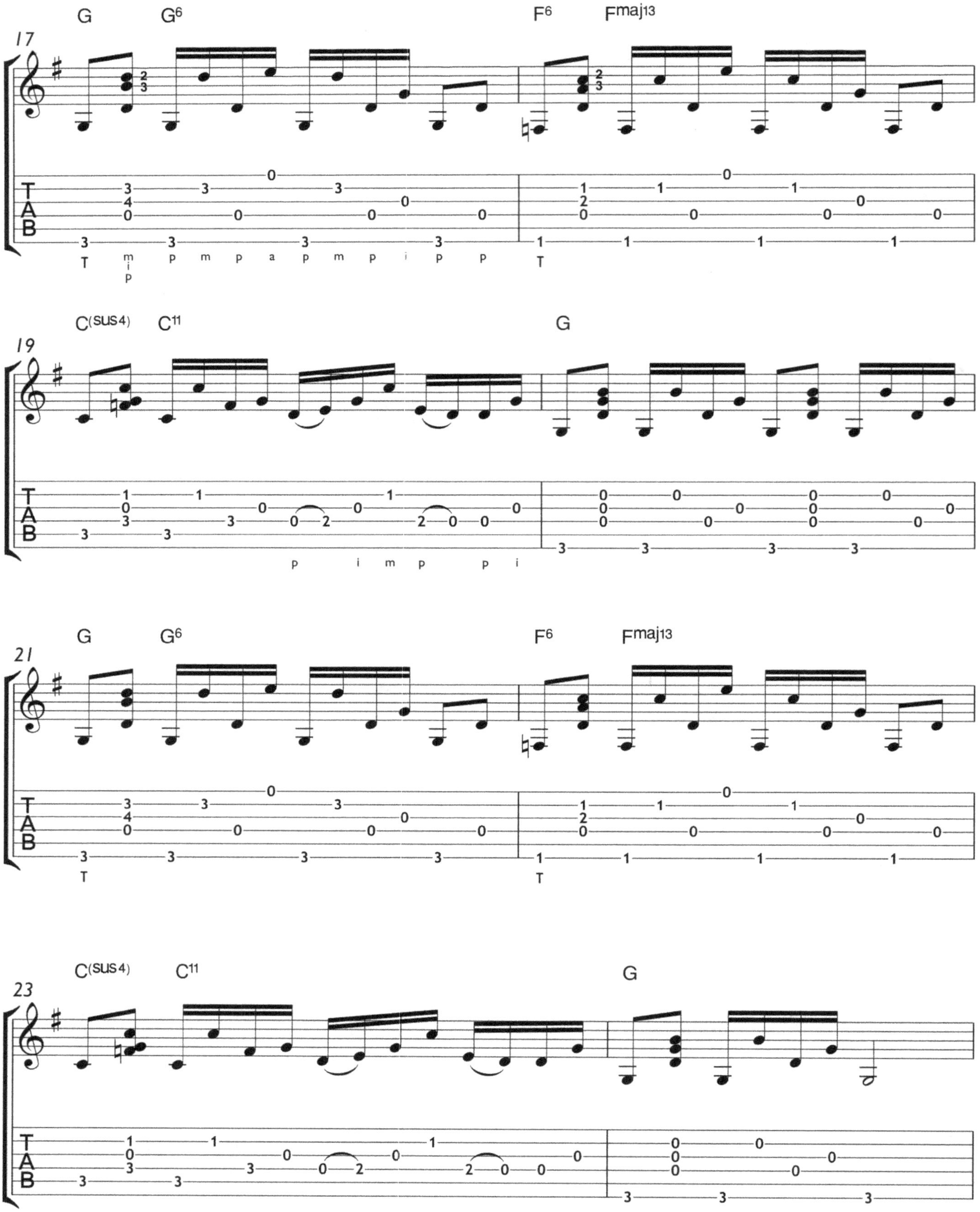
17
G
G6
F6
Fmaj13
19
C(sus4)
C11
G
21
G
G6
F6
Fmaj13
23
C(sus4)
C11
G

9
C(SUS4) C11 C(SUS4) C13
11
G5 G13(♯5) G5 G(add4)
13
D/F♯ C C13
15
G G7(SUS4) G G7(SUS4)

♩ = 84

Tuning = EADGBE

Capo Fret 4

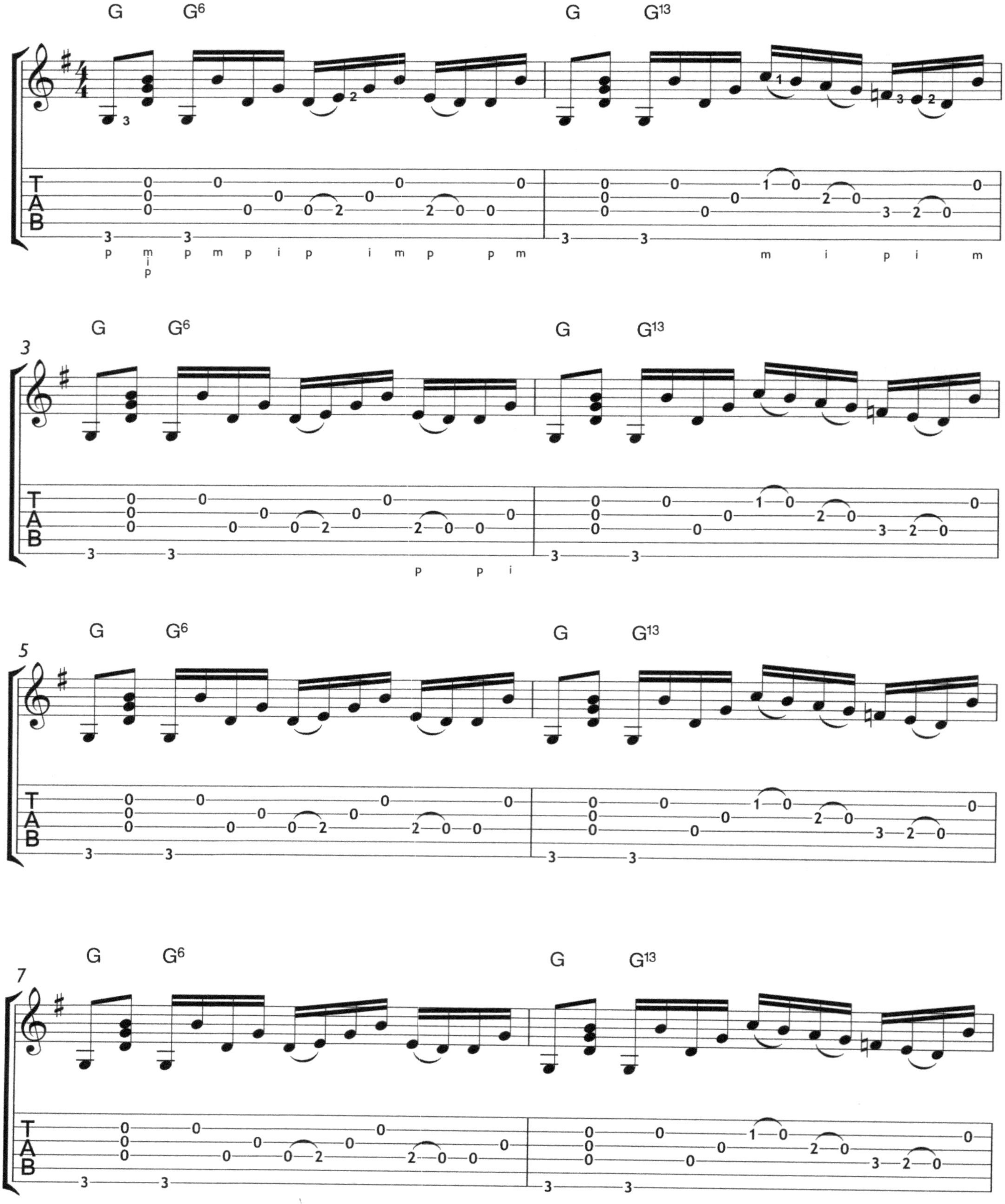

Bar 9 – Why play a major chord when you can play a sus4? Mayer has a great knowledge of chord voicings and how to use them. Alongside his technique it's part of what gives him his signature sound and you can learn a great deal from his approach to voicing and using chords.

Bar 13 – This type of phrase can strike terror into some players because Mayer is a thumb over the top guy! You can play these types of chords with conventional fingerings, but if you learn how to hook the fretting hand thumb over the top of the neck onto string 6 it will make these things a lot easier. (This is indicated by a "T" underneath the notation).

Bar 17 – Another thumb over the top idea. Again, it's not essential but it makes things smoother and can free up the fingers for embellishments on the top strings. It also means that you can play the open D and E strings as part of this chord.

Bar 26 – Another Mayer-esque chord at the end of this bar, a Csus2, is more subtle than the obvious C Major.

Shopping List

John Mayer has an enviable guitar collection to say the least. He has traditionally been seen with Martins of all shapes and sizes, but lately has been playing smaller bodied models, primarily his signature OM and 00-42SC (Stage Coach) guitars. If you are feeling really flush, then hunt out one the of 25 limited edition 00-45SC models that Martin made. However, you'll probably need to pay in excess of their original $14,000 price tag!

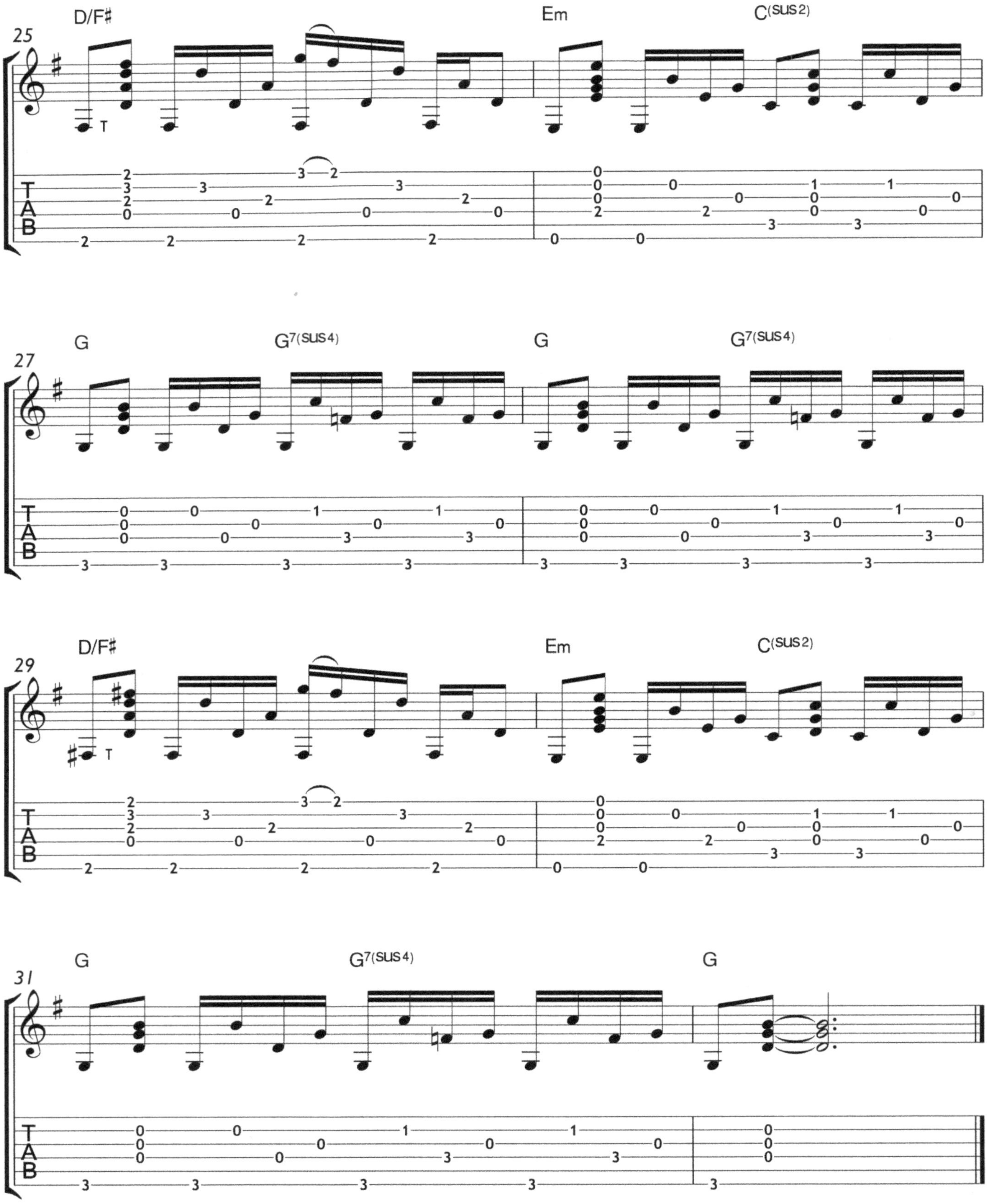
25
D/F♯
Em
C(sus2)
27
G
G7(sus4)
G
G7(sus4)
29
D/F♯
Em
C(sus2)
31
G
G7(sus4)
G

Chapter Ten: Noel Gallagher

Artist Overview

Born in Burnage, Manchester on the 29th May 1967, Noel Gallagher was inspired to pick up guitar after hearing the jangly guitar sound of The Smiths' Jonny Marr. Gallagher's guitar style is by far the most basic compared to the other artists in this book, but he is a great example of the singer-songwriter who uses the guitar as a rhythmic foundation for a track. Some players will decry Gallagher's lack of chops or musical education but it's important to remember that for many songwriters the guitar is a tool used in service of the song. Gallagher's masterstroke was to give his standard chord progressions something of a twist by incorporating subtle changes and additions to the shapes he plays. By keeping notes common to all the chords, he creates a unified sound throughout the well-worn Pop/Rock chord progressions and this serves to give them a fresh twist.

Play a simple open Em7 chord and watch your listeners' eyes light up as they think you are about to launch into that ultimate pub sing-along, *Wonderwall*! When you delve into Gallagher's playing you find that he has discovered a simple style that gives him a musical voice. Typically, a song will be based on a standard chord progression (sometimes with a jaunty, swing feel reminiscent of early Brit-rock icons like The Kinks) and hinged together by common tones – notes that appear in all the chords in the progression. *Wonderwall* is a case in point – the top two strings are sustained at the third fret throughout. Firstly, this surprisingly simple device yields some interesting chord voicings. Try playing *Wonderwall* with standard open Major and minor chords and see how much of the track's appeal disappears. Secondly, it allows Gallagher to keep his fingers in place on the frets and use them as anchors as he plays through a sequence. Another by-product of this approach to playing/writing is that you end up using chords that aren't so common in popular progressions, like 7sus4 chords and add9 voicings.

It's important to remember the value of keeping a strong, straightforward rhythm going when playing accompaniment parts, or parts that need to sit in a track and not intrude into the space of other instruments. Playing with a relaxed, slightly swung feel can be something of a challenge when strumming, so make sure you really lock in with the track when playing along with this study.

Listen and Learn: *Wonderwall, Talk Tonight, If I Had A Gun.*

Performance Notes

General Overview

It's all about solid rhythm and timing here, along with even dynamics and accuracy when changing chords. If you are new to playing along to a rhythm section, this study is a great place to start as the chord changes are not too hard and you can focus on your strumming hand and time-keeping. Remember, there is a light swing feel to the piece so you are not strumming with a straight rhythm. Keep the strumming hand loose and relaxed and aim for an even dynamic range so no chords jump out over others.

Bar 1 – We are following a simple strumming pattern here that is easy on the surface, but use it as an exercise in timekeeping, dynamics and accuracy. The Em11 chord at the end of this bar is not evidence of Noel's secret Jazz side, but the natural result of using all the open strings as a "bridge" to give him time to get his fingers ready for the following chord. You'll see a similar effect at the end of the next bar.

Bar 9 – Add9 and sus4 chords are quintessential elements of Noel's style. Much of this stems from the fact that it's easier to move chords around if the notes on the second and first strings (fret 3) are fretted all the way through. Plus, these chords sound great!

Bar 10 – Here's the aforementioned movement in action. Instead of playing a simple C – A – E progression, Noel will keep those notes on the top two strings fretted, which leads to a more interesting progression and he uses this a great deal in his playing and writing.

Bar 15 – Another common feature is the descending bassline featured here. The D/F# chord name makes it look scarier than it actually is. Again, this is a by-product of keeping those two strings fretted throughout and the descending bassline from G to F# simply means that we have a D Major chord with a major third (F#) in the bass.

Bars 23-24 – Noel doesn't just stick to standard chord progressions – occasionally he will play sequences like these that take the ear on an unexpected journey.

Bar 25 – The A7sus4 chord at the end of this bar is just another example of how transitioning from one chord to another while keeping fingers in place can yield some new voicings.

Shopping List

Early on in his career with Oasis Noel Gallagher can be seen playing Epiphone EJ 200 and Takamine acoustics. These days you will most often see him with a Martin D28.

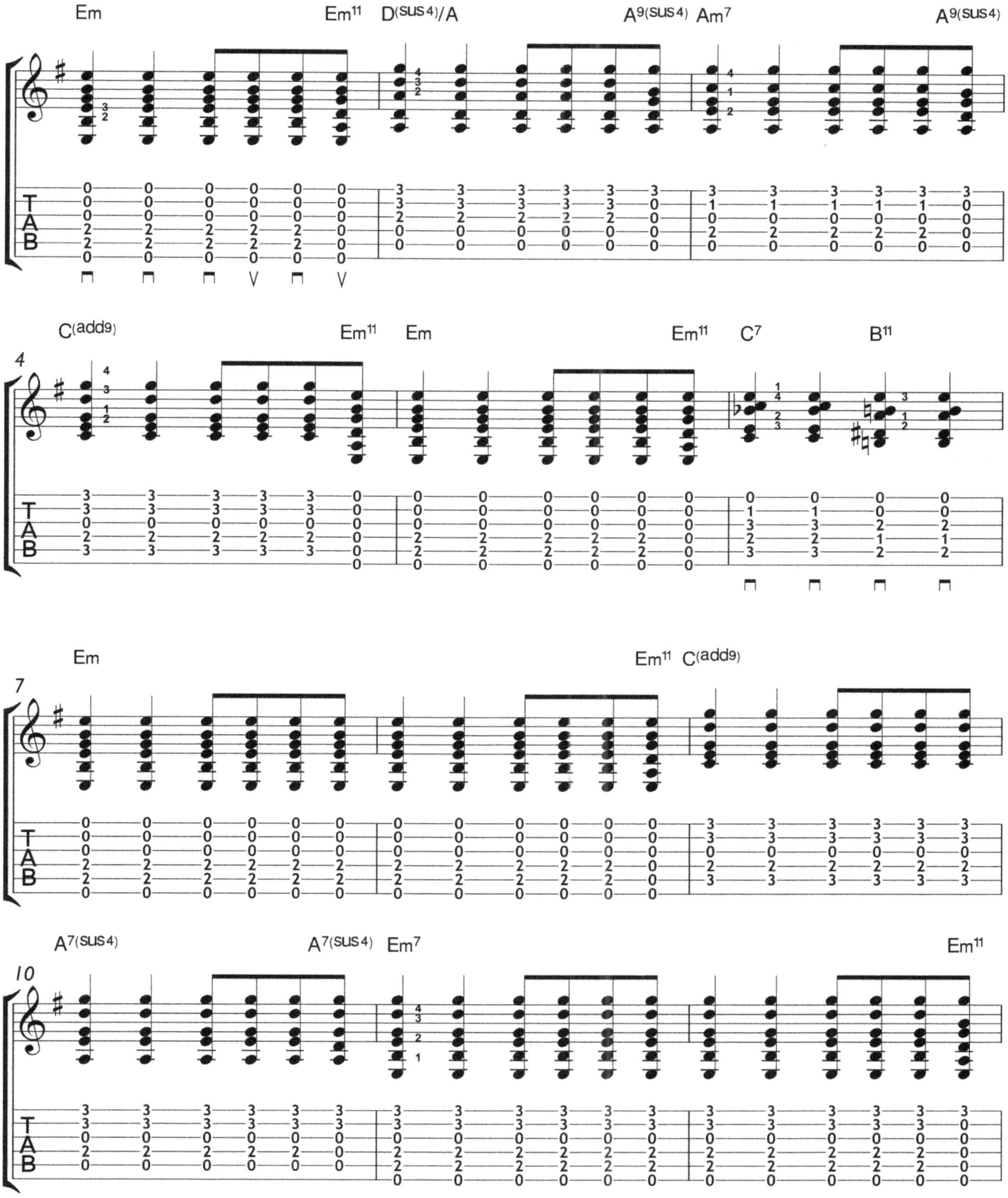

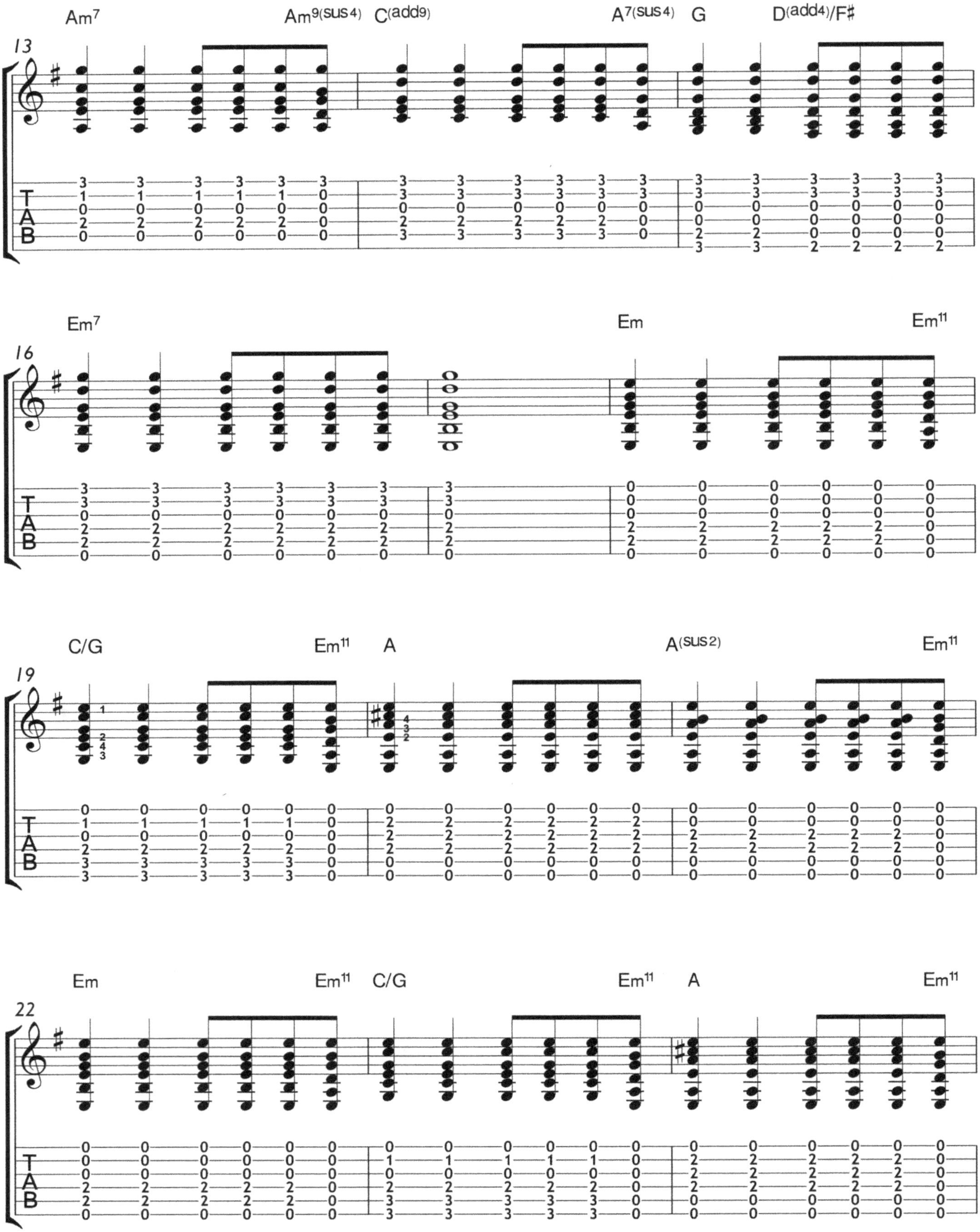
Am7 Am9(sus4) C(add9) A7(sus4) G D(add4)/F♯
13
TAB
Em7 Em Em11
16
TAB
C/G Em11 A A(sus2) Em11
19
TAB
Em Em11 C/G Em11 A Em11
22
TAB

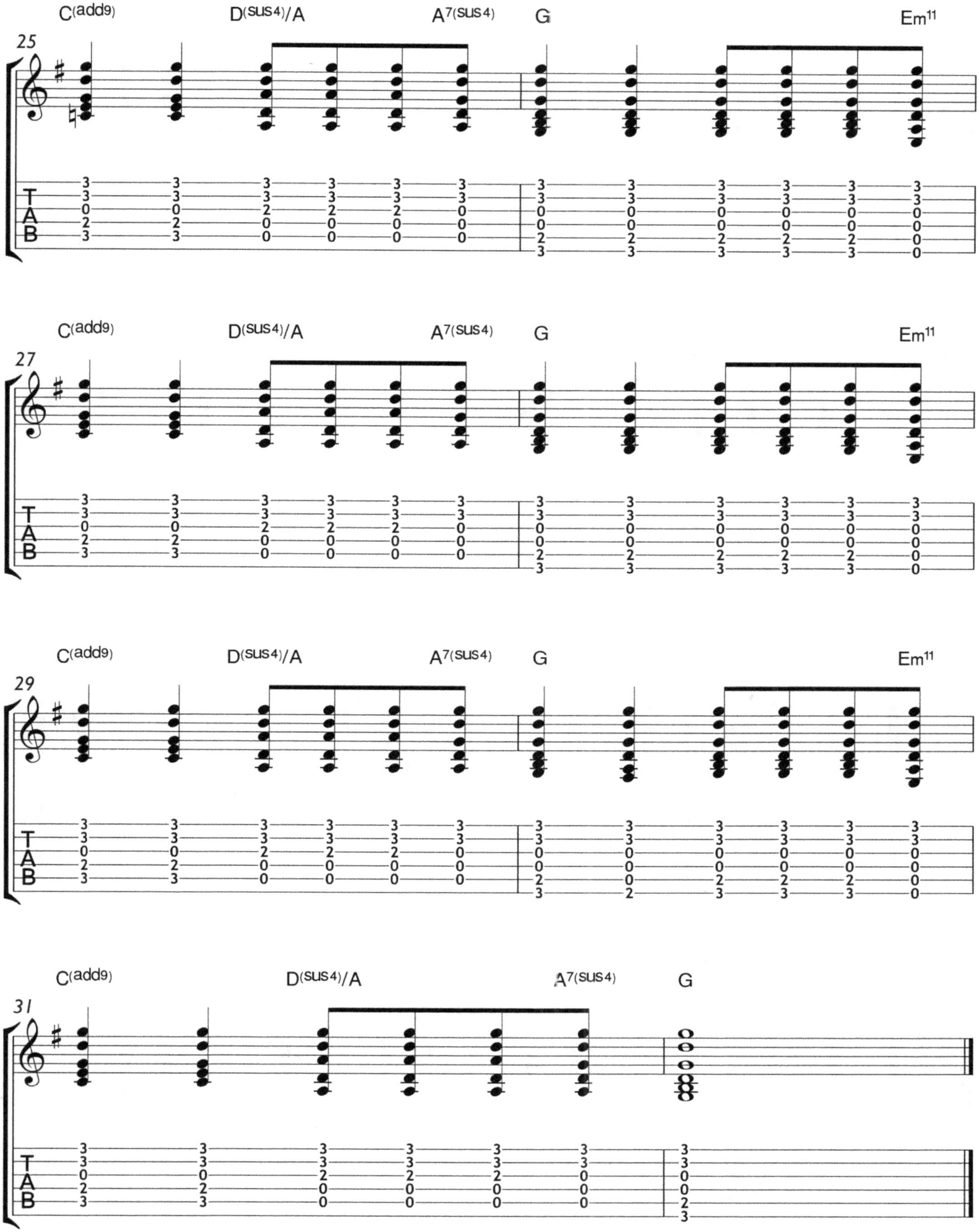
C(add9)
D(sus4)/A
A7(sus4)
G
Em11
25
T
A
B
C(add9)
D(sus4)/A
A7(sus4)
G
Em11
27
T
A
B
C(add9)
D(sus4)/A
A7(sus4)
G
Em11
29
T
A
B
C(add9)
D(sus4)/A
A7(sus4)
G
31
T
A
B

Chapter Eleven: Paul Simon

Artist Overview

Born on October 13th, 1941, in Newark, New Jersey, Simon's early musical influences were the star harmony vocalists of the day: The Everly Brothers and the Folk legends of the time, Leadbelly and Woody Guthrie. Listen to the latter two and you can hear how Simon developed his driving, fingerpicked accompaniment style, especially with the alternating bassline patterns so prevalent in Folk guitar styles. However, it is also worth noting that Simon was influenced by more "complex" guitar players of the day, including the UK's Davey Graham and Martin Carthy. Spending time in the UK, and in particular the "Café scene" of 1960's Soho, meant that Simon was around many of the great British Folk players of the day and this had certainly infused his playing when he returned to the USA.

Performing in a duo setting with Art Garfunkel meant that Simon's early acoustic guitar work was often at the forefront of everything they did. He always performed with clarity in his fingerpicking work, tight rhythm playing and a great command of dynamics, which meant his playing always supported their vocal harmonies perfectly. Famous guitar parts like those found in *The Boxer* show how Simon took on board the Blues/Folk styles of the time, complete with alternating basslines and deftly fingerpicked chords. As he developed his solo career, Simon began to create guitar parts with more advanced harmony that borrowed from the worlds of Jazz and Gospel. Check out the chord sequences to tracks like *Still Crazy After All These Years* and *50 Ways to Leave Your Lover* and you'll hear a different harmony to that found during the Simon and Garfunkel years. However, to really get a grip on his style, start with this earlier approach as it offers some great lessons in solid timing, the stamina needed to play through deft fingerpicked passages, and the importance of the alternating bassline to add interest when performing in a stripped back setting such as a guitar/vocal duo.

Listen and Learn: *The Boxer, 50 Ways to Leave Your Lover, Me and Julio Down by the Schoolyard.*

Performance Notes

General Overview

In this study we are going to take a look at Paul Simon's driving open chord playing. This was the key to tracks like *The Boxer* and *Homeward Bound*. There are several elements to work on here: first, the picking hand needs to develop the stamina and speed to keep the repetitive cross-picking patterns in place. Notice that for the most part, the picking hand pattern stays the same and the chord changes work around it. Keeping the timing tight when playing this style can be surprisingly difficult – you may find a tendency to rush ahead through the picking patterns, or find yourself lagging behind the backing track if fatigue begins to kick in. To get ready for this one, try playing it at a variety of tempos from slow to faster than the backing track in order to build strength and fluency in the picking hand.

Bar 1 – For this piece you can adhere to a traditional *pima* picking hand pattern using the picking hand thumb (*p*) to pick strings 6, 5 and 4 and the index (*i*) and middle (*m*) fingers for strings 3 and 2 respectively (there are no notes on the first string in this one so the "a" finger gets a rest!). Make sure you get the picking pattern in place by playing slowly at first, as this will remain the same for much of the piece.

Bar 3 – A classic Gospel-influenced approach is to play a Major chord with the 5th in the bass and this is what we have here with the C/G chord. This is common in Simon's guitar style and just means that instead of playing the root note (C) as the bass note you play the 5th (G) for a slightly different effect.

Bar 5 – Another common device used by guitar players of Simon's era was to play the 3rd of the chord as the lowest bass note. For the D chord in this bar, an F# (the 3rd) is played as the bass note on the second fret of string 6. This makes for a smooth descending bassline from the G in the previous bar (the third fret of string 6) and the subsequent movement to the open 6th string for the E minor chord.

Bar 8 – This pattern is probably the absolute embodiment of Simon's early guitar style – an alternating bassline from the root of the C chord to the 5th (G) that creates the illusion of a separate instrument providing the accompaniment. Though a simple device, in the context of a duo it's amazing how this adds movement and fills out the sound.

Bar 12 – This almost riff-based idea is another facet of Simon's playing. You'll hear this approach in his playing on everything from *Homeward Bound* to his challenging version of Davey Graham's *Anji*. Here the focus shifts to the fretting hand and strong, accurate hammer-ons.

Bar 29 – This passage echoes the technique of changing chords with a moving bassline found in bar 5. Here we use a short bass note run to move through the chords C Major to A minor to G Major.

Bar 38 – Make sure you change the picking hand fingers in this bar to play a D/F# and not the D7/F# that features in the previous bars.

Bar 46 – The focus shifts again to the fretting hand, this time combining a hammer-on to strings 4, 3 and 2 followed by a pull-off to the open strings. Hammering and pulling off several strings at a time does require some strength in the fretting hand, so if you haven't tried these ideas before, build them slowly so you can maintain the dynamic with the rest of the track.

Shopping List

Paul Simon has often been seen with a Martin OM42 and D18 and Martin also produced the OM-42PS signature model. While you'll often see him with Martin guitars, he is also a long time Yamaha user and has also used a Guild Songbird and an Ovation Custom Legend amongst others.

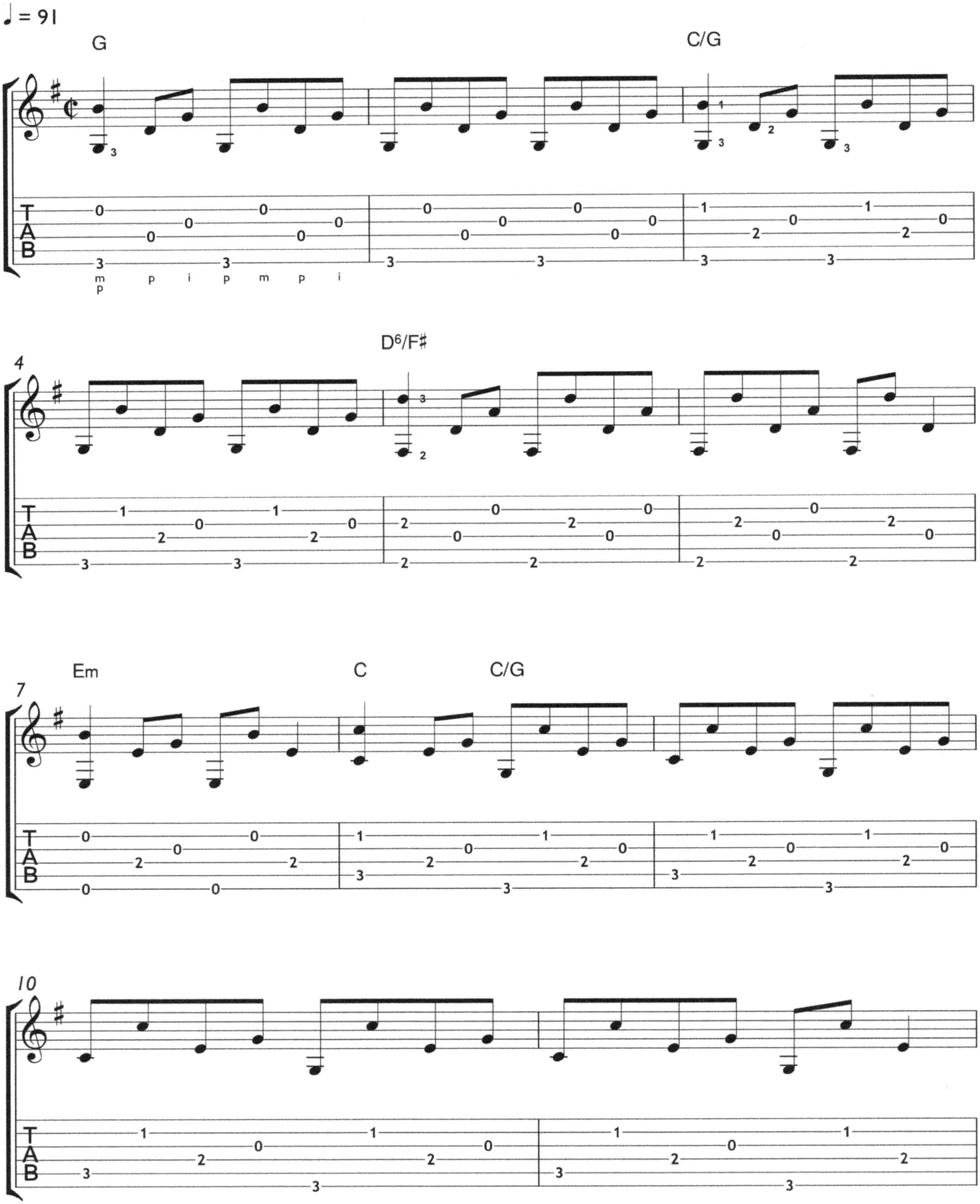
♩ = 91
G
C/G
m p i p m p i
p
4
D6/F♯
7
Em
C
C/G
10

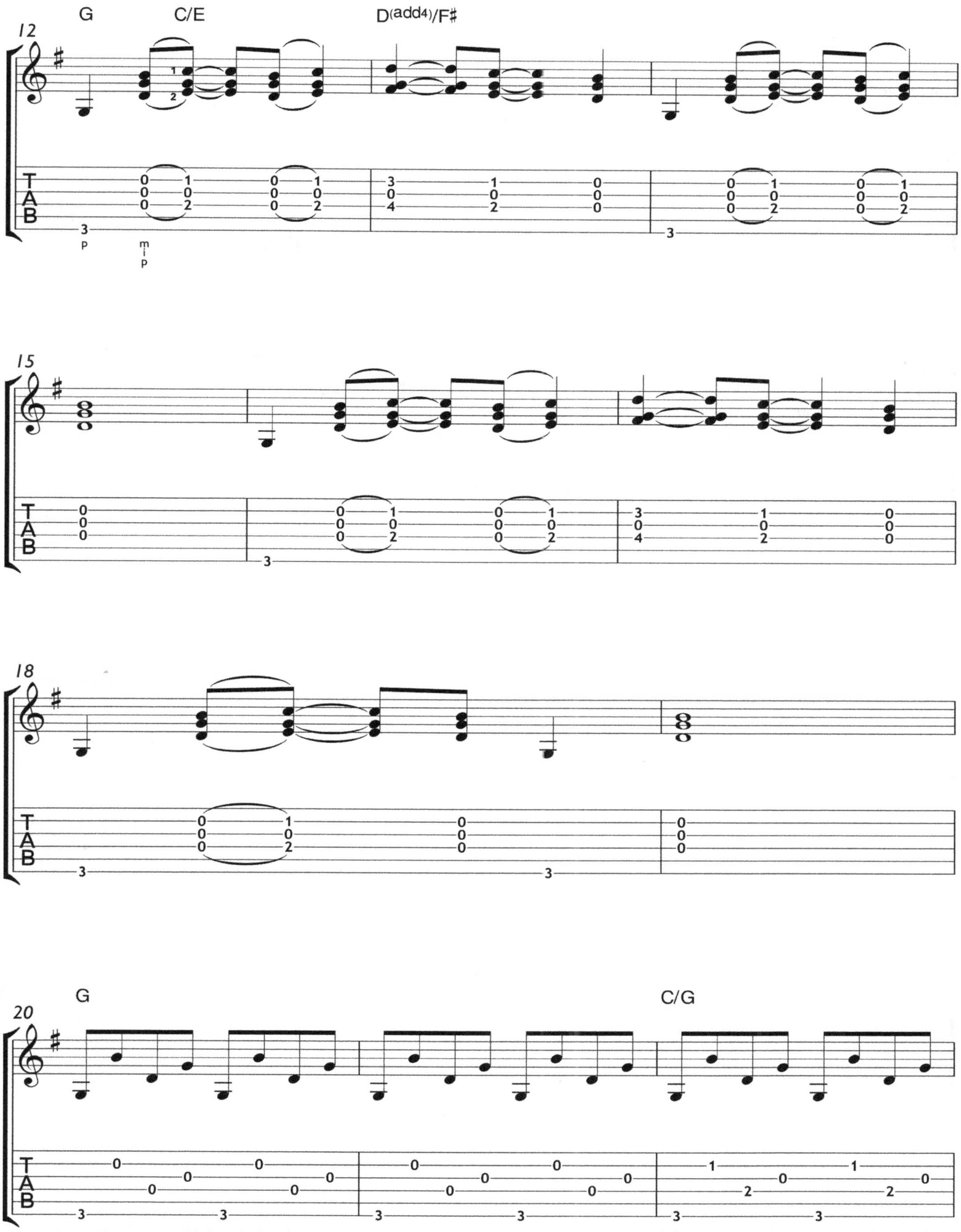
G
C/E
D(add4)/F♯
G
C/G

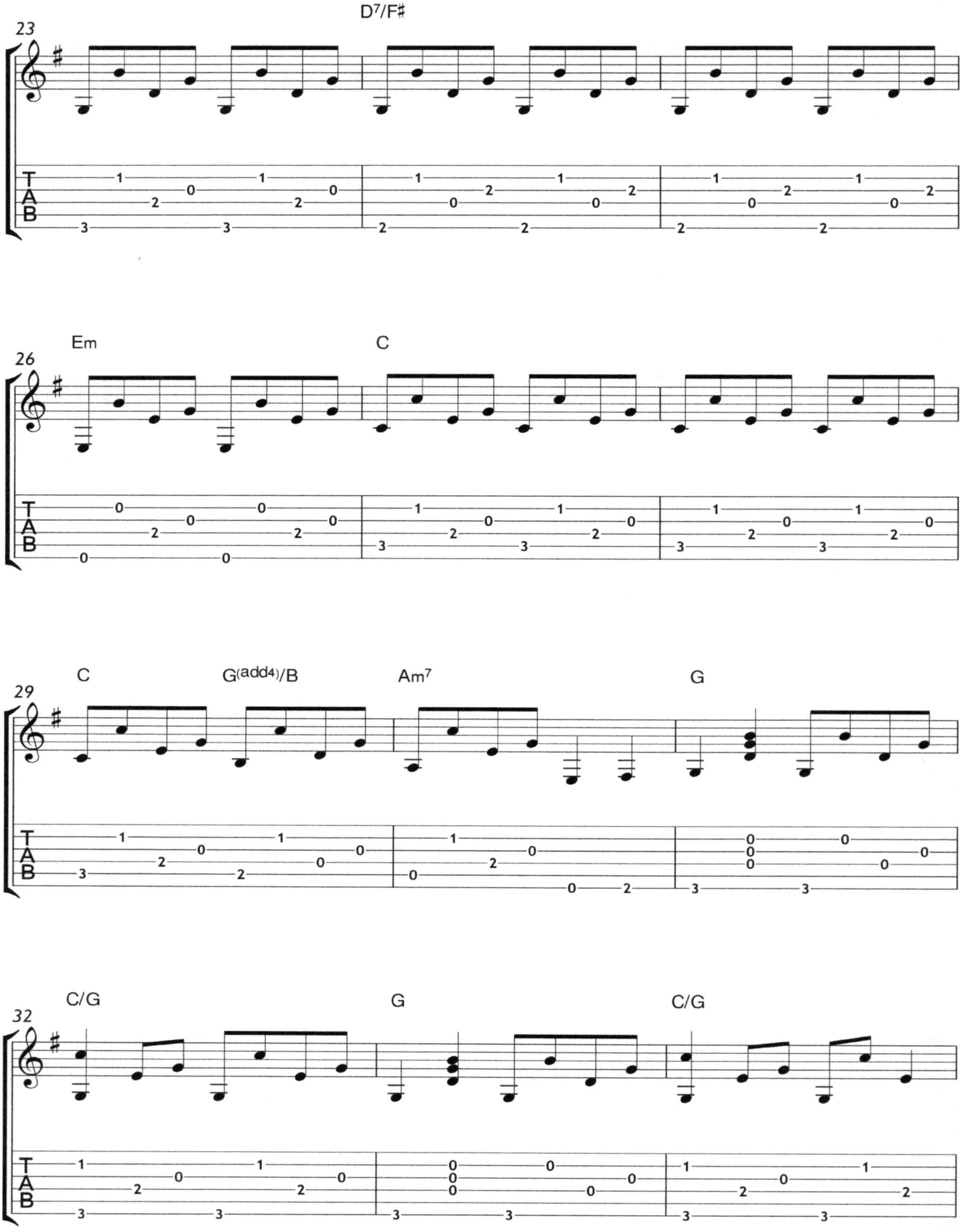
23
D7/F♯
26
Em
C
29
C
G(add4)/B
Am7
G
32
C/G
G
C/G

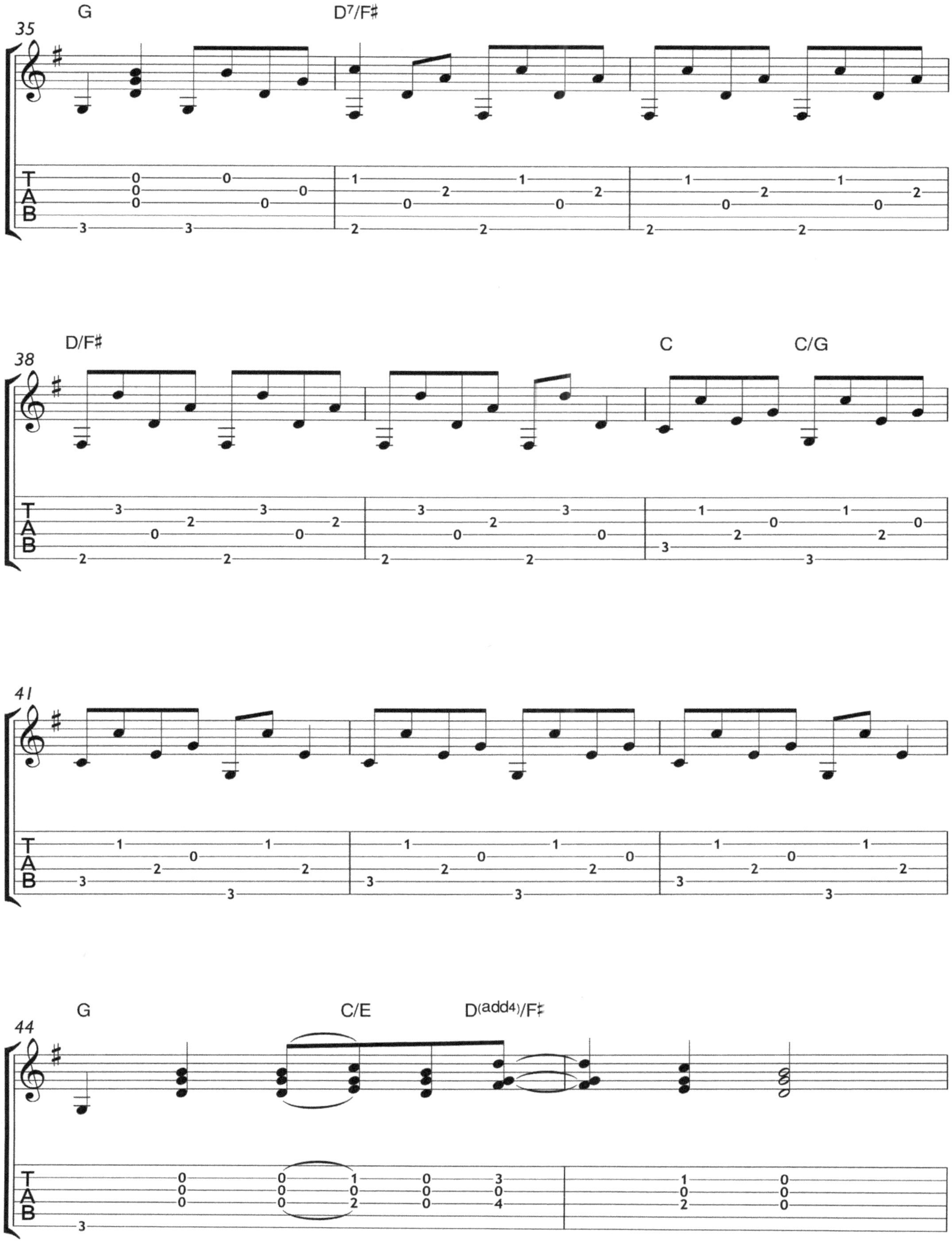
35
G
D7/F♯
38
D/F♯
C
C/G
41
44
G
C/E
D(add4)/F♯

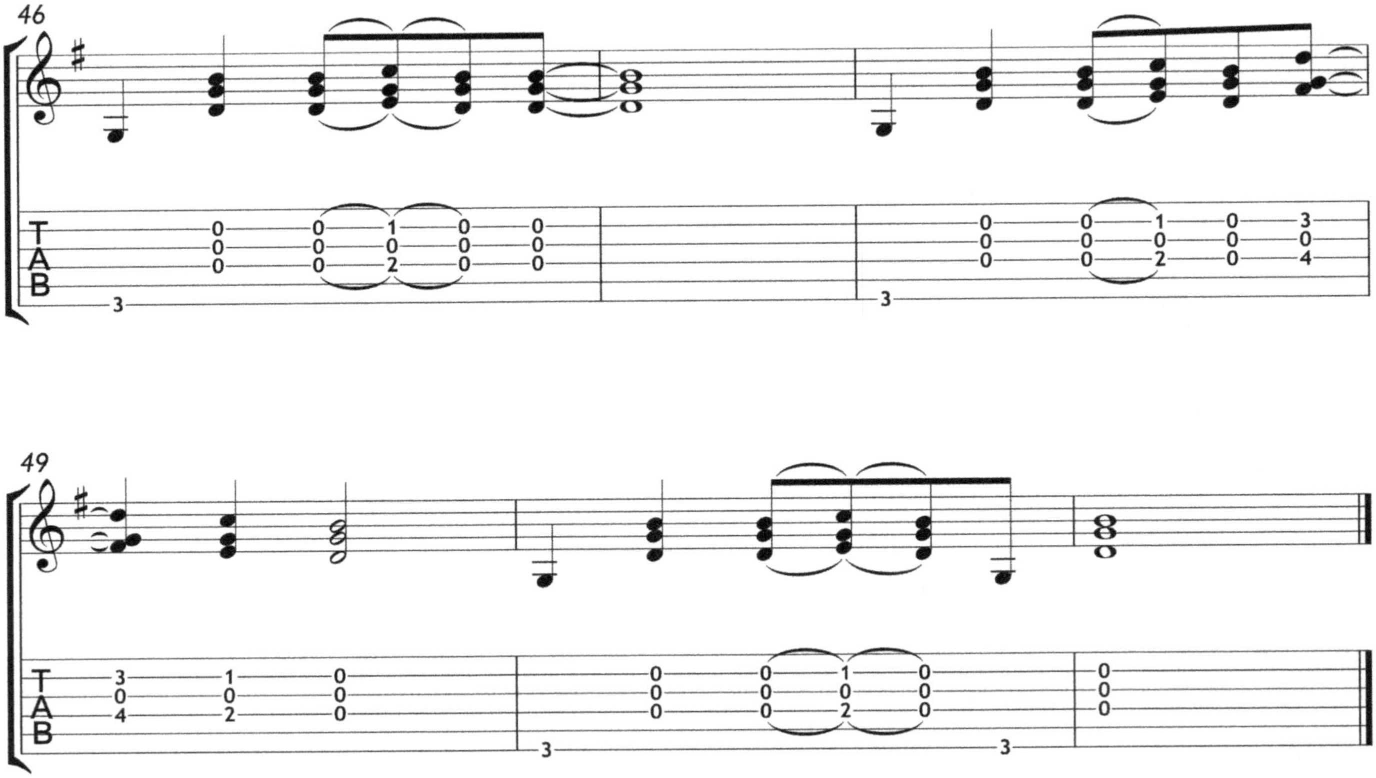
46
49

Chapter Twelve: Joni Mitchell

Artist Overview

Born in Fort Macleod, Canada, on November 7th, 1943, Joni Mitchell began her musical career busking and performing in small clubs in Toronto. She relocated to the US in 1965 and settled in Southern California where she began to write some of her biggest hits. Her talent as a songwriter was immediately obvious with classics like *Big Yellow Taxi*, *Chelsea Morning* and *Both Sides Now* heralding the arrival of an exciting new voice on the American songwriting scene. Other Folk artists quickly covered these songs and this served to spread her name and appeal even further. Her debut album *Song to a Seagull* was released in 1968 and followed by the 1971 classic *Blue*. During the 1970s her music took on a strong Jazz influence and she began working with future Jazz legends Pat Metheny, Jaco Pastorius and Michael Brecker.

As a guitarist, Mitchell has a unique approach to the instrument as the vast bulk of her songs feature an altered tuning. In fact, she has used over 50 altered tunings during her career! This study uses one of her favourites – CGDFCE – which yields some fantastic, Jazz-influenced chords. A big part of her writing style is the controlled use of dissonance, along with tension and release, and you will hear examples of this several times within this piece. I've used a capo at fret two for this one, something Joni often does herself. While the low tunings can sound great, they can also get a little muddy if you are not careful. The capo at the second fret adds a necessary touch of brightness and clarity when dealing with tunings like this one.

Mitchell has developed two interesting solutions to deal with the huge number of altered tunings she has used over the years. Firstly, and most practically, she has been using a Roland VG midi system since 1995, which allows her to programme in all the altered tunings without actually having to re-tune the guitar. Secondly, she has a fascinating system to remember tunings. For example, she would notate this piece's tuning as C77374. The first letter indicates the tuning of string 6 and the subsequent numbers tell her which fret to hold down on each string in order to find the pitch required to tune the next string.

Listen and Learn: *Morning Morgantown, Ladies of the Canyon, Little Green.*

Performance Notes

General Overview

In this study we are going to look at how an altered tuning can really shape a piece and provide the deep, rich chord voicings that are at the heart of Mitchell's acoustic style. You will also see how effective the open strings are in this style of playing – most of the chords only need one or two strings to be fretted to produce some fascinating chords. What's more, there are very few stretches and, in this study at least, no full barres. (Study Mitchell's work and you will find that index finger barres often do make an appearance). There aren't any challenges for the picking hand in this study and you can use the standard *pima* system of the thumb for strings 6, 5 and 4 and the *i, m* and *a* fingers for strings 3, 2 and 1. I've indicated some fretting hand fingerings, but go with whatever feels comfortable for you if my fingerings don't feel right.

Bars 1-2 – First, make sure you have re-tuned your guitar to CGDFCE and applied the capo at fret two. The short intro in bar 1 already suggests some of the possibilities this tuning presents. The chord at the end of the second bar is an example of how we can use some Joni-style tension before we play the main figure or verse section.

Bar 3 – This sequence is easy to play but the chords sound great thanks to the low altered tuning we are in. Often simply changing the bassline will yield great chords too and this is a common feature of Mitchell's guitar style.

Bar 8 – Unexpected chords and twists and turns in the harmony are other hallmarks of Mitchell's style. The Bb(#11) chord does not technically belong in this key, but it's a brief diversion from the conventional harmony and is another example of how she will bring unexpected tension into her guitar writing. The tuning is making chords like this immediately accessible without awkward fingerings or stretches.

Bar 9 – The Dm9 chord here is simply an embellished version of the chord we saw in bar 4. Use the index finger to hold down the notes on strings 6 and 5 at fret two and the second finger for the note on fret three, string 4.

Bar 27 – There are more rich chords here thanks to the CGDFCE tuning. There is also a bit of unexpected harmony via the move from F minor to D minor. Note how in bar 30 this reverts to the "correct" harmony for this key (F Major to D minor).

Bar 41 – There is more tension and release here as we progress from a chord within the key (Dm11) to one that doesn't belong (Eb6/9). This is all achieved simply by moving the bass note up a semi-tone from fret two to three and is another classic way that Joni gets movement and interest into her playing.

Shopping List

For the early acoustic years you will see Joni Mitchell playing a Martin D28. Later she moved onto electric and an Ibanez George Benson model alongside a custom-built acoustic by luthier Steve Klein. Most recently she has played a Martin D28, D45 and a Collings D2H.

♩ = 111

Tuning = CGDFCE

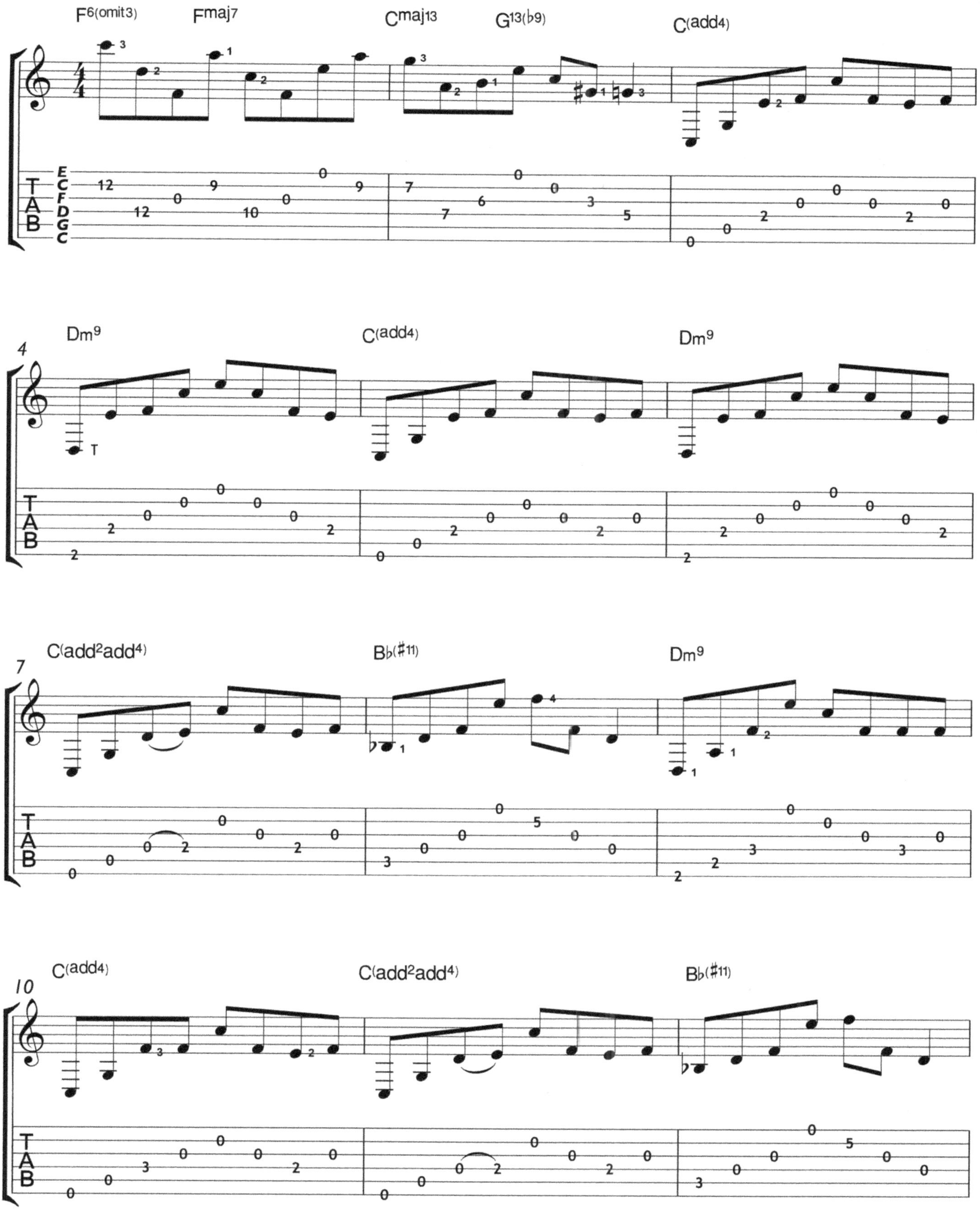

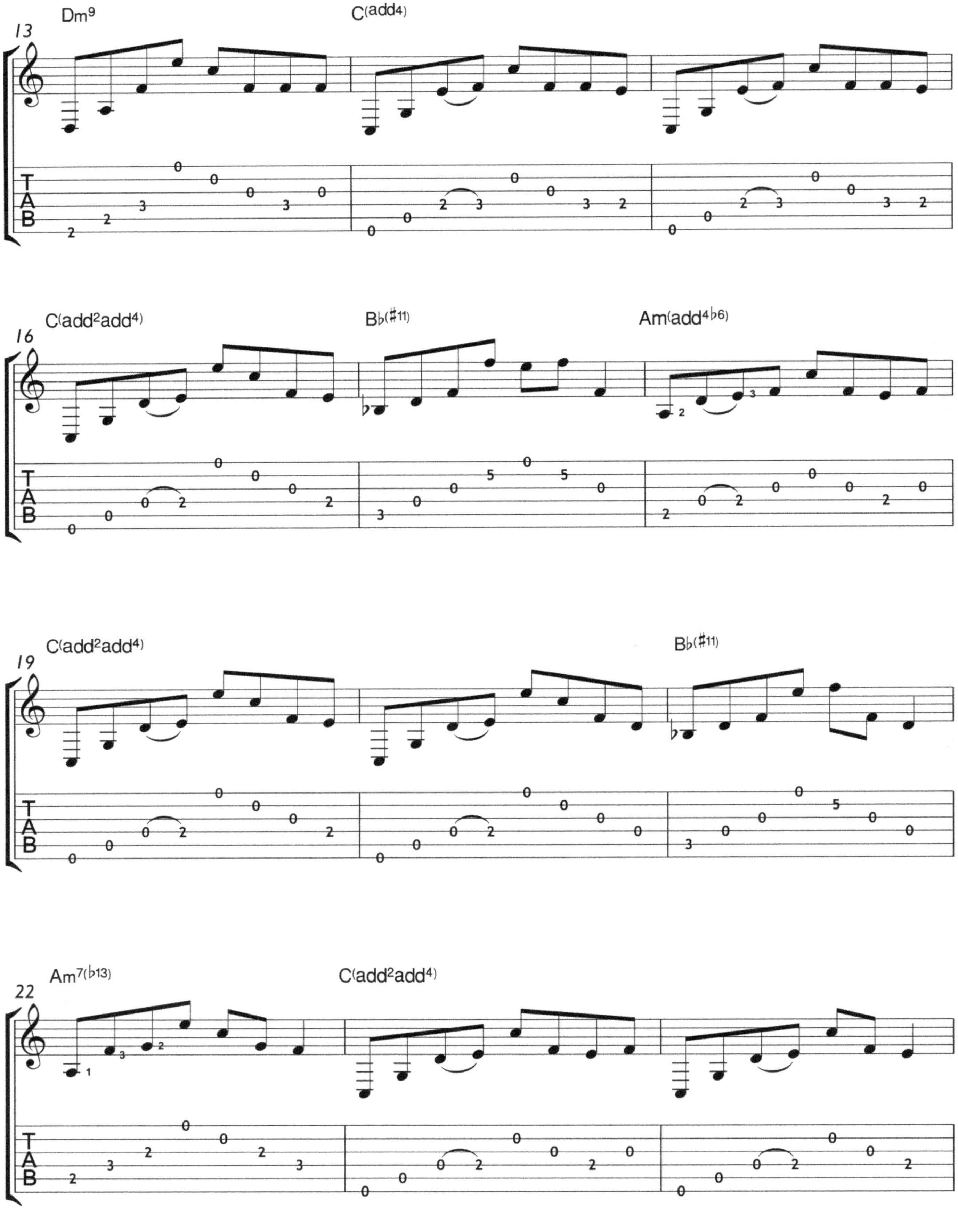
13
Dm9
C(add4)
16
C(add2add4)
B♭(♯11)
Am(add4♭6)
19
C(add2add4)
B♭(♯11)
22
Am7(♭13)
C(add2add4)

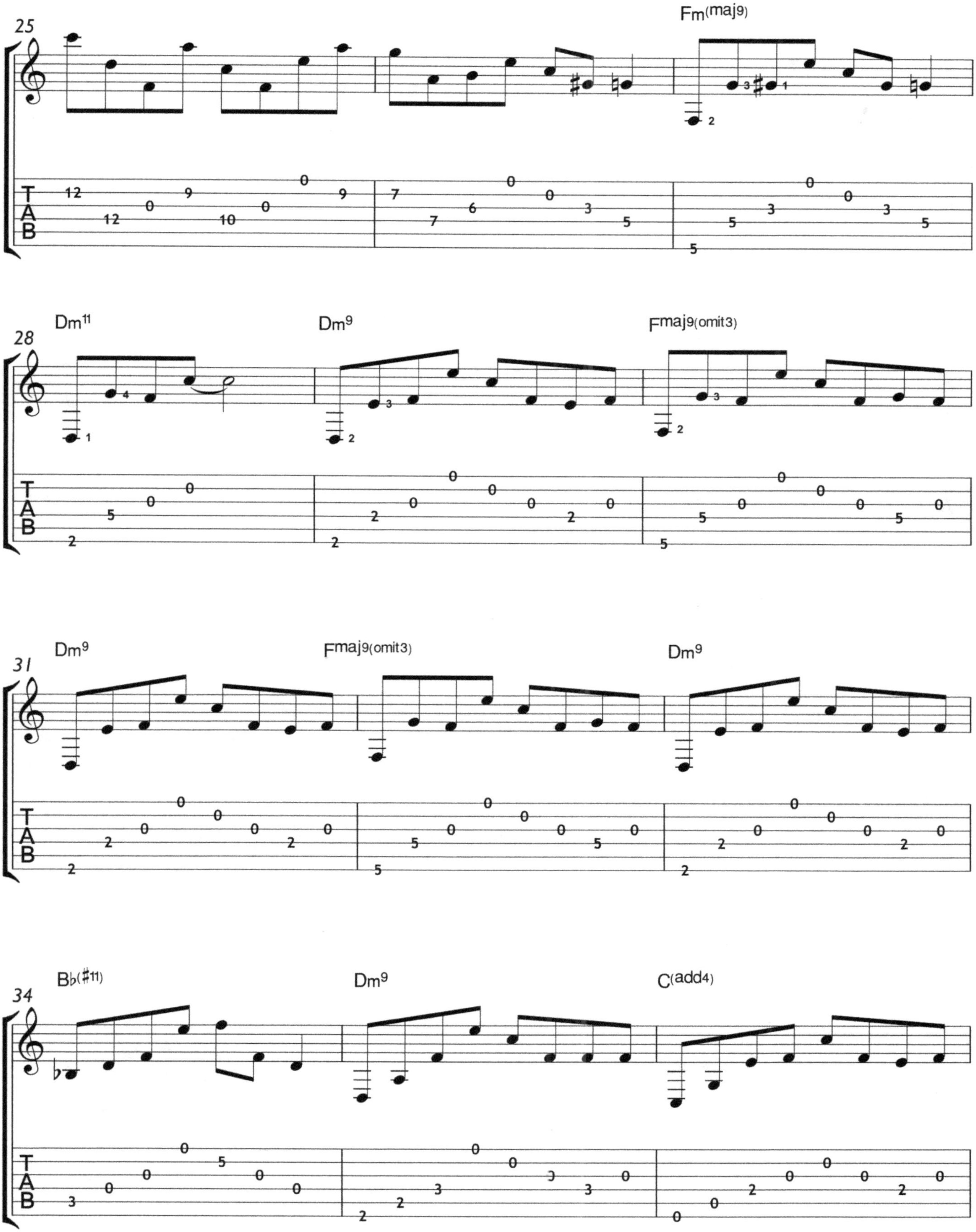
25
Fm(maj9)
28
Dm11
Dm9
Fmaj9(omit3)
31
Dm9
Fmaj9(omit3)
Dm9
34
B♭(♯11)
Dm9
C(add4)

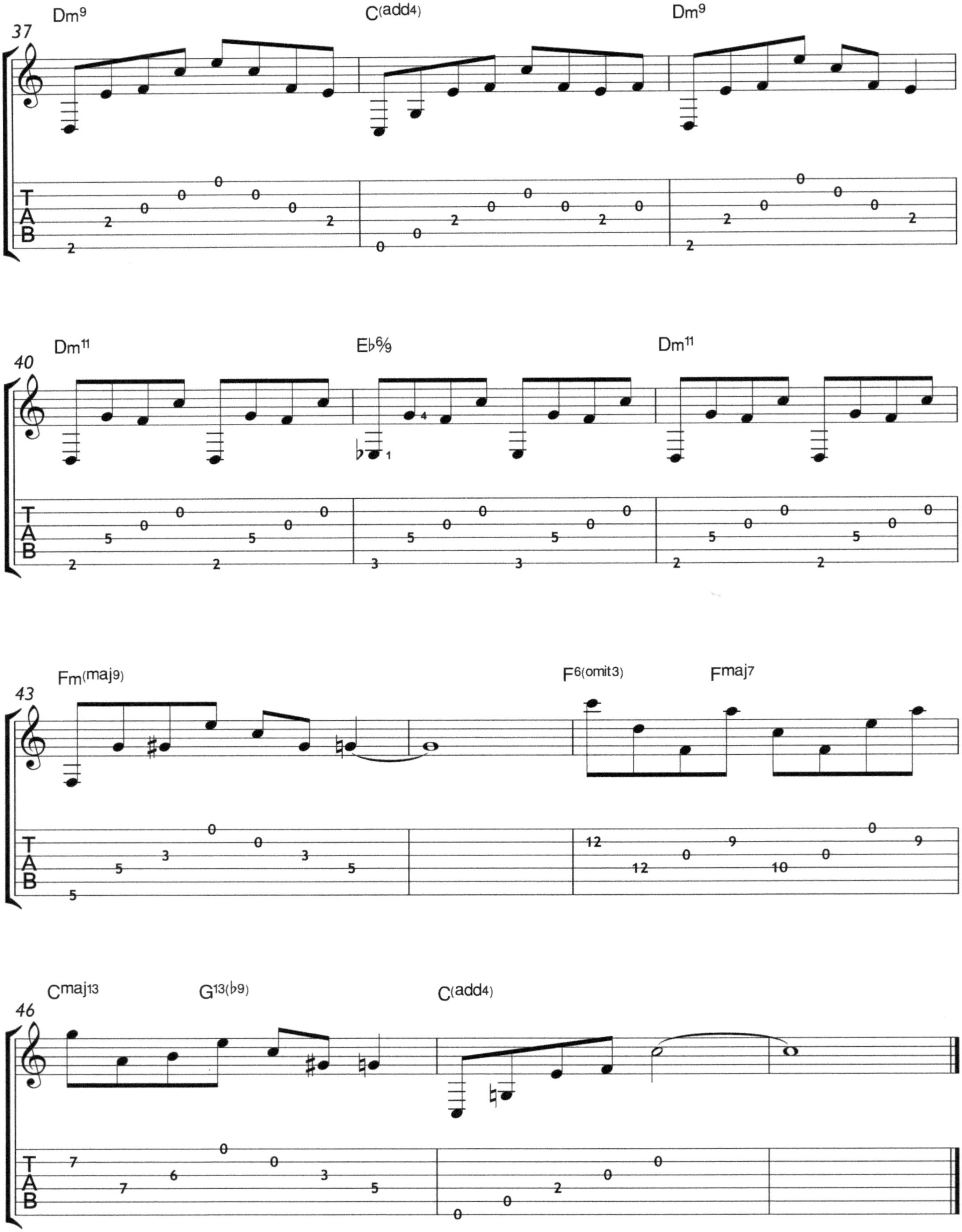
37
Dm9
C(add4)
Dm9
40
Dm11
E♭6/9
Dm11
43
Fm(maj9)
F6(omit3)
Fmaj7
46
Cmaj13
G13(♭9)
C(add4)

About the Author

"A world class guitarist, one of the finest of his generation."
–Martin Taylor MBE

"Will be one of the greatest guitarists this country has produced… a genius."
–Eric Roche

"That guitar sounds great in your hands!"
–Paul Reed Smith

"Super talented"
–Acoustic Magazine

"My friend Stuart Ryan is a fantabulous guitar player!"
–Jon Gomm

"My jaw dropped when you started playing!"
–Chris Difford (Squeeze)

Award winning musician Stuart Ryan is regarded as one of the UK's finest acoustic/electric guitarists. He began his professional career in 2002 when he was awarded *Guitarist Magazine's* Acoustic Guitarist of The Year and cemented his reputation with countless live appearances at concert halls, guitar festivals and clubs across the UK and Europe. A personal invitation by Martin Taylor MBE to appear at his Kirkmichael Guitar Festival in 2003 brought Stuart to the world stage and since then he has been busy as a concert guitarist, studio musician and author.

With a wide range of influences from rock guitarists to traditional blues and folk musicians and everything in between, his versatility has kept him busy and in demand. His solo guitar concerts take in everything from the haunting sounds of traditional music to the unbridled joy of African Kora alongside his own compositions and arrangements of well known pieces.

Follow Stuart's monthly tuition columns in *Guitar Techniques* and *Guitarist Acoustic* magazines. Discover more at **https://www.stuartryanmusic.com**

The Legends of Acoustic Guitar

Learn to play guitar in the style of the world's greatest singer-songwriters

ISBN: 978-1-78933-200-1

Published by **www.fundamental-changes.com**

Copyright © 2020 Stuart Ryan

Edited by Tim Pettingale

www.fundamental-changes.com

Twitter: @guitar_joseph

Over 11,000 fans on Facebook: **FundamentalChangesInGuitar**

Instagram: **FundamentalChanges**

For over 350 Free Guitar Lessons with Videos Check Out

www.fundamental-changes.com

Follow the author:

https://www.facebook.com/stuartryanmusic/

https://twitter.com/stuartryanmusic

https://www.instagram.com/stuartryanmusic/

https://www.youtube.com/user/StuartRyanMusic/

Cover Image Copyright: Shutterstock – dindumphoto

THE**LEGENDS**OF ACOUSTIC**GUITAR**

Learn to Play Guitar in the Style of the World's Greatest Singer-Songwriters

STUART**RYAN**

FUNDAMENTAL**CHANGES**